THE JOURNEY UP

by the same author

The Journey Up

Reminiscences

1934-1968

MAURICE COLLIS

London
FABER AND FABER

First published in 1970
by Faber and Faber Limited
24 Russell Square London WC1
Printed in Great Britain by
Latimer Trend & Co Ltd Plymouth
All rights reserved

ISBN 0 571 09000 1

In Memoriam
matris meae dilectae
Edith Collis
Obit MCMXLIX

CONTENTS

9

Contents

ILLUSTRATIONS

I

How I left Burma

In EARLIER MEMOIRS of mine, *The Journey Outward, Into Hidden Burma* and *Trials in Burma*, are sketches of childhood in Ireland, education in England and how in 1912, aged twenty-three, after passing into the Indian Civil Service, I was posted to Burma, then a province of the Indian Empire. Some account followed of life as an administrator in the Burma of those early days. *The Journey Outward* ended with 1917–18 when I went to Egypt and Palestine with the first battalion to be raised of Burmese troops and got back to England after an absence of six years. *Into Hidden Burma* covered the years 1919 to 1934, the date I retired from the Indian Civil Service, aged forty-five, hoping to make my way as a writer. The third book, *Trials in Burma*, is a detailed account of experiences when I was chief magistrate of Rangoon in 1930–1. Now in January 1969, at the age of eighty, I set out to complete the survey and explain how after some twenty-two years in Burma as a Civilian (a member of the Indian Civil Service was so termed) I managed to enter the literary world of London.

Civilians were men of first-class education. It was impossible to pass into the Indian Civil Service without having secured high honours in the degree examination at a university, at that time generally Oxford or Cambridge. A Civilian had the same official standing as a member of the Home Civil and Diplomatic Services. He could aspire to a knighthood, even eventually to the governorship of a province of the Indian Empire, an appointment comparable to that of Assistant Under Secretary of State in

London or, if a diplomat, that of Ambassador. But it was more difficult for a Civilian to keep up his education and move with the times. Stuck for years in little country towns with nobody of quite his education to mix with, and much cut off from the world of ideas, he tended to fall behind his contemporaries in London. His concern was all with the people in his jurisdiction. He grew fond of them, tried to be fair, toured the villages, listened on the bench to complaints and petitions, and became immersed in the details of district administration, interesting work enough but not such as to furbish the brains which had enabled him to pass into the Indian Civil Service. He got duller than he was at the start and came to believe it was his mission in life to take care of and instruct a backward oriental people. This amiable misconception, comparable to a missionary's, gradually stultified his intellect. He had little perception of the trend of world events. In my time the most striking example of this was the case of Bernard Swithinbank. A classical scholar of brilliance, a double first at Oxford where he also won the coveted Craven scholarship, he was one of Lytton Strachey's intimate friends, and as an associate of the Bloomsbury set, was well placed to meet some of the most gifted young men and women of the period. He knew Maynard Keynes very well and Virginia Woolf and Arthur Waley. But he chose to become a Civilian in Burma, much to the dismay of Lytton Strachey. None of his senior colleagues there quite grasped what it meant to have frequented such circles. The importance of his contemporary outlook was not appreciated. His talents were not made full use of. He was confined to the routine of district administration, and had little influence on the inner councils of the government. But he was not unhappy; as a recluse, reading in particular the Latin classics and discharging his duties with careful diligence, he was content. As may be supposed, the Burmese had his sympathy in their desire to regain control of their country. But as a district officer nothing in that line came his way; there was nothing practical he could do to aid them. The Civilians who controlled the government's policy at the capital, Rangoon, knew well enough that he was not their man. As an able administrator he had no doubt to be promoted, but always to appointments in the countryside. He got the small title of a C.B.E. in 1938. On retirement, aged fifty-eight, in 1942 (by which date Burma was lost to the Empire), he was taken into the centre and made Adviser in London to the Secretary of State for Burma, a post he held for four years. He was not knighted, perhaps because all was over as far as the Indian Empire was concerned. And he wrote no books.

His case may be compared with that of George Orwell (an old Etonian like himself) who was for a time his contemporary in Burma. Orwell was not a Civilian but a member of the Imperial Police. The academic requirements for that service were similar to those needed for entry into the British army. But though he had little of Swithinbank's literary background he had a more downright character and less indulgence for out-of-date views. He was able to bear the tediousness of the British bureaucracy in Burma for only six years (1922–8), when he resigned and threw himself into the literary career which made him famous. His first book, a novel, *Burmese Days*, can hardly be termed a work of much literary merit. It is a carpentered affair. But it vividly reveals his reason for leaving Burma. The British bureaucracy, Civilians and others, were intolerably boring for a man of his intellect. Their ideas belonged to the previous generation. Fervent admirers of the Victorian conception of empire, they did not share the enlightened opinion that Burma should be liberated from the foreign domination under which it had fallen in 1885. In his novel Orwell gives a scorching picture of their mentality. He was fundamentally at variance with their way of thinking. There was no career for him as an official. He was in the wrong place. His feelings were so strong that he sacrificed a good income and a pension, resigned from the police and for a time was down and out in London and Paris.

My case can in some ways be compared to Swithinbank's and Orwell's, though I was luckier than either of them. When I entered the Indian Civil Service I had no strong feelings for or against the Victorian conception of empire. A Civilian's job was well paid, seemed novel and exciting and independent. But I discovered that it did not really suit me. I was not sufficiently interested in administration as a subject. I was not keen enough on the work. I wanted, of course, to get on, but was unable to identify myself with what would have recommended me to my seniors in the service. I was not the industrious careful type. And I grew too fond of the Burmese and sympathetic to their aspirations to be fancied in high quarters. Anxious to please, I tried to conform, but could not keep it up. From as early a date as 1919, when after the 1914–18 war I was on leave in Europe for a year, I began to wonder how I could get out of the Civil Service and make a career as a writer in England. But I had not the courage to take the plunge. With a family to support, it would indeed have been idiotic and cruel. Besides I had nothing solid to go on. I had a longing but what gifts? After making the acquaintance in 1922 of the Dublin literary set, particularly James Stephens and A.E., I tried my hand at verses on the Irish heroic cycle and even got published a thin volume of poems on themes which had already inspired Irish writers. I had some encouragement, but there was too much fancy and too little common sense in my aspirations.

My yearning, however, for a literary outlet remained strong. In 1924–5, when I was deputy commissioner of Akyab, it took a more promising turn. I was enabled, with the help of an Arakanese scholar of the most charming character named San Shwe Bu, to write a number of historical essays on the old kingdom of Arakan and Mrauk-U, its magical capital. My friend, Gordon Luce, a distinguished poet and scholar, a member of the Burma educational service, had these articles published in the *Burma Research Journal*, a periodical of which he was then editor. All told, the articles ran to 20,000 words. At that time Sir Harcourt Butler was Governor of Burma, a man of wider outlook than any of his predecessors in that appointment. He wrote and congratulated me. His recognition was an event of great importance for me. These articles were to be the basis upon which my later book, *The Land of the Great Image* (published 1943) was founded. The reaction of my immediate superior, the Commissioner of Arakan, was to complain to the Chief Secretary that the articles were proof I was neglecting my official

Geoffrey Faber at an editorial lunch in 1944'

Mrs. Samuel White's tombstone at Mergui.
Painting by Gérard Laenen, 1932

duties. I had no warrant to interest myself in the past when I was paid to oversee the present.

But having the Governor's blessing I was immune. Indeed, the articles did me professionally some good, for I was called to the Secretariat in Rangoon and made Deputy Secretary to the Chief Secretary. Flattered by a posting which put me right in the centre of affairs at the age of thirty-six, I began to view my work with more interest. Could I not combine my literary and artistic inclinations with a successful official career? I worked hard, did my best, and tried to believe that if the Government of India was contemplating, as rumoured, a grant of limited self-government to the Burmese, persons like myself with liberal views would have their chance. There were vague signs that such a change was coming. But it might be long before the old order yielded place. My first interest in secretarial routine began to flag. I now doubted making a success that way.

On leave during most of 1927 I again sought means of escape. I had remained in touch with my old friend of school days, Geoffrey Faber, who had gone into publishing. In 1927 it so happened that he was planning to buy out Gwyer, his partner at that time, and found the firm of Faber & Faber, where he would be free to develop his own ideas. He offered me the post of director in the projected firm, provided I put up a substantial investment. It was a dazzling offer. I would move straight from exile into the centre of London life and letters. But I could not find the money for the investment. I would have to stay on in Burma for another decade before I got my pension of £1,000 a year. It was idle to imagine that I could resign and support my family on the earnings of an author.

After coming to this hard conclusion, I found consolation during the remainder of my leave in familiarizing myself with modern art, especially in Paris, where I knew some painters. I became also captivated by Chinese ceramics, and bought a number of pieces both in London and Paris. It was possible at that date to buy, if you hunted round, such objects of art for one tenth of their present price. Loaded with these purchases and altogether much better informed, I returned to Burma.

A few months later I was made head of the magistracy in Rangoon. I had no idea that this appointment was to carry me a step nearer my ambition to become a writer. I was still in the good books of the government, considered perhaps a little too indulgent to Burmese aspirations, but otherwise competent to take charge of the law courts of the capital. As there was a whiff of reform in the air, it was not necessary to be so downright imperial as before. But the senior officials and the commercial community remained very old fashioned. Some change was inevitable, of course, but the longer it could be postponed the better. I had no idea that what might seem to me a normal discharge of my duties on the bench would seem to them so gravely disturbing as to put an end to my amiable hope of making a success of my official career.

What happened is fully described in my *Trials in Burma*. Officially I did for myself by delivering three judgments upsetting to authority, though in accordance with the law. I had no chance ever again of promotion or appointment at the centre. I would be quietly buried in remote country places. At the moment I did not grasp the full bearings of the matter. I did not apprehend the complete incompatibility of my outlook with that of the reigning party in Rangoon. Far less could I perceive that I was actually on the threshold of the fortunate half of my life. How naïve had been the notion that I could do well as a Civilian, how sound the intuition of a career of letters. But at the moment, 1931, none of this was clear. It was only evident that if I resigned I got no pension. If I stayed, there would be no prospects. I was apparently faced at forty-two with either poverty or an official cul-de-sac. But I kept up heart. And gradually a solution was revealed. Fate in a curious intricate pattern disclosed what to do and how to do it.

During the years of my Rangoon magistracy I had spent part of my leisure writing verses, inspired not by the Irish heroic cycle but by occasions when my emotions were engaged. I enjoyed the close friendship of a few talented friends. I wrote a number of fanciful pieces which were published under a pseudonym in the local press, as I had no wish to give umbrage to the old guard who viewed my literary excursions with distaste. These served to keep my eye in. By a lucky chance I was able to pursue my interest both in painting and in Chinese ceramics. No one in Rangoon, not even the orientalist Gordon Luce, had studied Chinese ceramics. But lying in the open market, mixed up with modern bowls and dishes, were pieces of antique porcelain. The prices were very moderate. Ten rupees (13s. 4d.) went a long way. My study of the subject in London and Paris enabled me to go ahead with some confidence. Being only a beginner I made mistakes, of course, but managed to add to my existing collection quite a number of authentic examples, including a few imperial specimens. The experience I gained in this way worked in curiously with the lucky pattern which was evolving as will appear.

After a leave of six months in the second half of 1931 I returned to Burma. The government, which had had more than enough of me at Rangoon, resolved to send me as far out of the way as possible and chose Mergui, a fishing port on the Bay of Bengal, unconnected with Rangoon by motor road or rail, and distant a voyage of two and a half days by sea. Yet in this unlikely place everything essential to start me on my new career was to be provided.

An old trade route was known to have existed from Mergui eastwards across to the gulf of Siam. That this route had been used in previous centuries by exporters of Chinese porcelain on their way to the Indian, Persian and Egyptian markets was not on record; even the ceramic experts of London and Paris were unaware of the fact. A mere chance led me to identify the old porcelain route. A local tin miner, Mr. Hand, when dining with me one night in my house at Mergui said, after looking at my Chinese collection, that in the course of his mining operations he had come across fragments of apparently the same sort of wares. I immediately visited his mine and saw lying among his tailings a lot of porcelain fragments dating from the twelfth to the eighteenth centuries. It struck me that if such quantities of fragments were turned up in his tin washings, whole pieces would come to light somewhere along the old trade route, if inquiry were made. I let it be known among the villages that I was ready to pay for any such. Nothing happened until the people got to know me better. The villagers for years had occasionally unearthed bowls, plates and cups when ploughing or pulled them out of the river in their fishing nets but they kept quiet about it, for they believed they had occult or magical properties. A man known to possess such might come under suspicion of plotting rebellion, for with their aid he could render himself invulnerable. Moreover, in general to have objects of a supernatural kind about the house was alarming. Accordingly the practice was to present such pieces to monasteries or let the buffaloes stand on them. But now, when they heard that for reasons unknown I was prepared to buy antiquities they cautiously produced a few. Since no ill effects resulted they became bolder. A search was made for more pieces, monasteries were not averse to exchanging what they had for money. People had dreams and dug and found caches. In the course of a year it had become a trade. Volunteers scoured the jungle for more. Sometimes old women were unwilling to sell antique cups, having found that medicine drunk from them did more good than from ordinary cups. But this was exceptional. Everyone was glad to sell to me and might come two days' journey by boat to do so. It was remarkable that they never made a mistake. They could tell an antique piece as well as any London dealer. They had the eye of persons who all their lives had handled old pieces. Perhaps their impression of occult force was not wholly different from the aesthetic reaction of a connoisseur.

The pieces being rather rough export porcelain were not potted and decorated with the same skill as those I had bought in Rangoon. Their importance, as I was to learn, lay more in the fact that their discovery proved the existence of a hitherto unknown trade route between the Far and Middle East, and showed the sort of porcelain wares which were exported that way.

The authorities in Rangoon, on my reporting that I was collecting antiquities, were not pleased, on the same ground that my articles on Arakan had displeased—I was wasting my time. It is hard now to believe this; indeed, I did not guess it at the time. They did not write forbidding me to continue to add to my collection, but their letters had a pernickety tone that warned me I was irritating them in some way. Not till long afterwards, when speaking to a Governor who succeeded the then Governor, did I learn that he had found it recorded in my confidential file that my ceramic investigations showed a lamentable lack of keenness in my work. There was one ridiculous sequel here. The Commissioner of Tenasserim, my immediate official superior, came down from his headquarters 250 miles away to inspect. By that time my collections were considerable, a couple of hundred pieces perhaps. When he saw what I had bought, he himself became bitten with a desire to make a collection. He let it be known that he would pay liberal prices and succeeded in getting some pieces which my people had intended to offer me for sale. After a fortnight's stay he went off satisfied and spoke up for me thereafter. I should, perhaps, have been grateful to him, but I was not. He was too silly a man.

These transactions in the field of Chinese porcelain were to have more significance for me than I realized at the time. An account of them was to interest the London public as was another matter, now to be related. The two together launched me on the life to which I had long aspired.

The other matter was the subject for a book. So far I had not found a subject I could manage. But now quite unexpectedly one was put into my hand. I owed this to a Mr. Archie Forbes, a proprietary rubber planter and tin miner. One evening at the little club bar he spoke to me of Samuel White, a Bath adventurer, who had lived in Mergui in the sixteen-eighties. His story, declared Mr. Forbes, 'is extraordinary. What I know of it comes from a few pages in Anderson's *English Intercourse with Siam in the Seventeenth Century*,' a dry academic work written thirty years back and forgotten. This was more interesting than the usual talk in the club. Forbes had the book and lent it to me. When I read the bit about White I suddenly saw my chance. Here I was in Mergui, my house on the very site of White's, below it the harbour where the climax of his drama was enacted

in 1687. Anderson had no literary talent whatever, but he had
unearthed the elements of an astounding tale. No one could have
been in a better position than myself to elucidate it. In the course
of my duties, without hurry or fear that the authorities in
Rangoon would call me to order, I could explore the terrain
associated with White, the islands, the mangrove, the lonely
river, and find out the possibilities of a biography.

From that day on I visited every place within reach connected
with his name. I was able to do more than a man in England
working from the authorities listed by Anderson could possibly
have done. But if my book—for I already saw it as a book—were
to be really good, I had of course to read the original papers on
which the narrative rested, which were all in London. In Mergui
I did what could be done, but I could not write a line till I had
read the authorities. I had come upon a story, of historical importance, original, extraordinary, and if I could write it might
make my début. But I could not be sure I was capable of the
task. And I could not be sure, even if the papers in London were
as interesting as they promised to be, that I could risk leaving the
service. It remained a gamble. Would it not be more sensible to
stay on, write the book on my next leave and only decide if its
reception was encouraging? Moreover, constitutional reforms
were in the offing, which would give the Burmese more
authority in their country. When the reformed constitution was
inaugurated surely I could hope for a career in Burma which
would suit me. These various reflections gave me pause.

Such was the state of things when in October 1934 I was
granted a year and three months' leave on half pay and went
home. Shortly before I left the India Office amended the service
rules, a change which turned what for me hitherto had been a
gamble into a feasibility. It was decided to give Civilians the
option of retiring on proportionate pension; it would be unfair
to expect them, under the new constitution, to serve under
Indian (or Burmese) ministers. I saw that if I retired at the expiry
of my leave I should have a pension of £900 a year, which
would just suffice if supplemented by royalties. It was true that
to get this proportionate pension I should have to declare my

reason for applying was in accordance with the Secretary of State's kind intention to spare me the indignity of serving under a Burmese minister. But apparently the declaration was a mere formality; if you wanted to retire you could do so, whatever was actually your reason.

When I left Mergui in October 1934 I had, however, not finally made up my mind to retire in January 1936 when my leave would be up. Better to wait and see a bit longer. I was so undecided that I did not take my collections with me. All my antiquities, my paintings, my books and papers were packed and stored in the Mergui customs; the officer in charge undertook to despatch the boxes later, either to England if I retired or to wherever I might be posted in Burma. My mind wavered, for I was fond of the Burmese and many of them were much attached to me. Before my departure the inhabitants of Mergui presented an address, in which they begged me to come back. I was moved by this and other tokens of affection and left Mergui actually in tears.

My family was in Dublin. Early in 1935 we left Dublin for London and rented a house in Adelaide Road, N.W.3. To write a biography of Samuel White I had to be in easy reach of good libraries. I had nothing but a footnote in Anderson's history to tell me that the diary of White's secretary, Davenport, the most vital of all the sources for White's story, was in the India Office library. When I presented myself there in May and asked to see the diary, I was informed by a librarian, after an interval, that it could not be found. Much dashed by this, for all my hopes were founded on getting the diary, I inquired whether a search could be made, and was told to call again in a week's time. The people I spoke to were very offhand. I departed much depressed. However, when I returned, the book was produced. The diary had been printed in 1687, along with other papers, for official use in a law suit. I will never forget the emotion I felt on my first glance through the pages. I felt quite sick with excitement. The volume could not be taken out and I spent part of the month in the library copying out the diary. As I read, all fell into place. I had hoped for a good thing, but what I found exceeded all expectations. By June I was sitting in a room in the Adelaide Road house and beginning to write as fast as I could.

Having been out of London since 1912 except for short visits during my leaves in 1918, 1921, 1926 and 1931, I knew few people. Besides my old friend Geoffrey Faber, who by 1935 was turning his firm of Faber & Faber into a leading publishing house, my acquaintance with people of standing was very limited. One of them, however, was my uncle, Sir George Grierson, to whom I now turned for advice. He was eighty-four years of age, an O.M. and incontestably the most famous expert on the languages of the Indian Empire and such adjoining countries as Tibet and Siam. His *Linguistic Survey* of those languages in eighteen volumes displayed a fantastic familiarity with the structure and relationship of 179 languages and 544 dialects. Other publications of his were very extensive and included some translations of Indian classics. He was much liked by Indians of all classes. When the Maharajas came to London on a visit they used to call on him, bringing presents. He lived at Camberley in a quiet way. I went down to visit him on 10th June 1935. I draw the description which follows from notes made at the time.

'Uncle George, having recently had bronchitis, was in bed. I was ushered into his room by the nurse. The old gentleman was a wonderful sight, propped on his pillows. The pundit of all oriental pundits, he lay with a gold-embroidered cap on his head. (This was a present from the Gaekwar of Baroda.) A beautiful ancient expression played on his face. His white beard fluffed round. He looked like a pastoral king, noble and benign. I approached with respect. My enquiries about his health were turned aside, but he spoke of a translation of Sanskrit tales which he was preparing for publication by the Asiatic Society. "The Society," said he, "have the proofs. There is a little difficulty. Some indecencies occur in the text, not obscene of course, but just a trifle blunt. The Asiatic Society has rules about pornography. But they have left it to my discretion. What do you think, Maurice? Should I omit certain words? In primitive courts prostitutes had the entrée." I ventured to reply that one should not tamper with a classic text. Perhaps the Asiatic Society was a little Victorian. He seemed satisfied, though he withheld judgment. I then told him about Samuel White and Davenport's diary and how my intention was to attempt something with them. Speaking with an endearing serenity he said: "There is no one more fitted than yourself to carry through such a book." By this time I saw he was tired. As I withdrew he bade me farewell in a rich deep tone as if uttering a magical blessing in Sanskrit.'

He had hinted I should join the Asiatic Society, which I now did and met there some members, notably Reginald Le May, Quaritch Wales and Sir William Foster, who were leading authorities at that time on the matters covered by my projected book.

It was the right moment to call on Geoffrey Faber. I had not seen him for three and a half years, when he had introduced me to Lionel Curtis, who gave the Burmese delegates, in London to discuss with the British government a future constitution for Burma, useful advice. Faber's position in London was now imposing. Fellow and Bursar of All Souls and shortly to be made President of the Publishers Association, chairman of Faber & Faber's brilliant staff of directors, among whom was T. S. Eliot, he was on the way to a knighthood. Had I not known him since he was fourteen, he might have dazzled me. As it was I was just delighted to see him again. I rattled off my news and told him I was writing a book on a certain Samuel White which seemed to promise well as an exciting story. I hoped that when he saw it, he would take it. He was not much impressed. One is not impressed when an old friend, hitherto unknown in the world of letters, announces at the age of forty-six that he is writing his first book, about a man no one has ever heard of. He did not, for instance, warm to the idea and offer me an advance, nor had I the knowledge of the book trade to ask for one. But he was cordial and kind and I went away satisfied that if I finished the book and it seemed all right I could send it to him, sure he would do his best to take a favourable view.

So with the aid of the India Office library, the library of the Asiatic Society and the advice of some of its best-informed members, I threw myself enthusiastically into the composition, determined that I would not be tedious, would always cut a long story short, would choose the best bits in the sources and leave out the rest and aim at a style cleansed of all traces of the official jargon in which I had been obliged to write my reports as a Civilian.

I did not give my whole day to this task. There was the matter of the Mergui trade route and its porcelain which I wanted to bring to the ears of the right people. Though I had left behind my collection in the Mergui custom house, I had brought with me some forty fragments, representative of the whole. I knew none of the big collectors of Chinese antiquities and none of the museum people had ever heard of me. Of the dealers in Chinese wares I had met the two Bluett brothers and now went to their shop in Davies Street, one of the three best of its kind in London. Besides the fragments, I took with me some rough photographs of what I had got in Mergui. In a note made at the time I record: 'The Bluetts considered many of the pieces were 14th and 15th century, and some earlier still. In their view I had a definite contribution to make to the study of oriental ceramics and should write a paper on the subject.' On my inquiring how to go about this they told me that the paper should be read to the Oriental Ceramic Society, to which belonged all the big collectors and leading dealers, including themselves. In token of their interest and desire to help, they rang up Bernard Rackham, Keeper of the department of Chinese ceramics at the Victoria & Albert Museum, and brother of the famous painter, Arthur Rackham. An appointment was made for me to call, which I did on 11th May 1935. He was a man of sixty and about to retire after thirty-seven years' service in the department. His publications were numerous and he was beyond question an expert on Chinese ceramics of the calibre of R. L. Hobson of the British Museum. He received me with a politeness which I found soothing after the attitude taken up by the powers in Rangoon. On examining my fragments and photographs he said that the Bluetts were right in suggesting a paper before the Oriental Ceramic Society and that he himself would address its secretary, the Hon. M. W. Elphinstone, on my behalf.

I was so miserably out of touch with London connoisseurship that I did not half realize the compliment that was being paid me. I knew nothing about the Oriental Ceramic Society and on leaving Mr. Rackham with many expressions of gratitude, prompted more by good manners than by understanding, looked up the list of the members of the Society's council. Its president was George Eumorfopoulos, the millionaire ship-owner, whose vast collection, not only of oriental antiquities but of European works of art, had made him world famous. At about this time he sold part of his Chinese collection to the British Museum for £100,000, pieces of such rarity and excellence that not a million pounds could buy them today. Among his colleagues on the Society's council were notabilities like Alan Barlow, Sir Percival David, Professor Seligman and Mrs. Walter Sedgwick. (The residue of her collection after bequests to the British Museum and private legatees was sold at Sotheby's for some £170,000.) It was before these erudite connoisseurs and the members in general of the Society, among whom were other noted collectors, such as the Crown Prince of Sweden, that I, totally obscure, accustomed to the disapproval of my seniors, and for the last twenty years mentally starved in the Burmese jungles, was invited to express my views for a full hour. That I found nothing astonishing in the notion shows that I was either horribly conceited or childishly innocent.

In conjunction with my work on the book I began writing the paper, to be read before the Society on 9th October 1935. During these four months I got to know George Eumorfopoulos. When informed of my discovery of porcelain on the Mergui route, he wrote to me at once, showing great interest and asking me to lunch at his house on the Chelsea embankment. I happened at the moment to be in Paris having a look at the Siamese antiquities in the Guimet Museum. His letter was forwarded, but when I opened it I could not read his signature, which was comparable in its illegibility to the Chinese grass hand. After a while, however, I guessed he must be the writer and gratefully accepted. I recorded in my diary a note on this first meeting with the great connoisseur. 'I was shown by the maid into the drawingroom which was lined to the ceiling with glass cases full of porcelain of the highest quality. Mr Eumorfopoulos came in, a little man in black, very old and very foreign looking, with a deep voice. In a few instants he was joined by his wife, a Greek too, I think, and we went down to lunch. There were just the three of us. I noticed that all the china on the table was antique, the plates and bowls being of the reign of the Emperor K'ang Hsi. After lunch I went with Mr Eumorfopoulos to his study and discussed with him my projected paper. He approved of what I had in mind.

'I now perceived that his appreciation of the arts was far wider than that of a specialist in oriental ceramics. His study was full of modern sculpture, pieces by Mestrovic, Epstein, Skeaping, Eric Gill, and other sculptors of note. There were also in his study examples of modern stonewares; I noticed pots by Staite Murray, Leach, Vyse and Miss Pleydell Bouverie.'

From the above it would seem that I had already acquired some smattering of the work of the new school of studio potters then rising to fame. That I was not totally ignorant, pleased Mr. Eumorfopoulos and he took me on a tour of his house. 'Leaving the study we strolled into the hall, where I noticed a 14th century Ayudhyan Buddha with curly eyebrows. There was also quite a collection of modern paintings on the walls.'

These paintings were by English and French artists then coming into vogue. A long Stanley Spencer caught my eye, high over a doorway. He had recently finished the Burghclere frescoes. Eumorfopoulos's wonderful eye had enabled him to pick out artists later destined to become famous. I remember hearing with amusement some members of the Ceramic Society deploring his aberration in filling his walls with such paintings. Any sort of modern painting was anathema to the general run of ceramic enthusiasts. Though they enormously admired Eumor, as they called him, they thought in this matter he was wasting his time. I seemed to have heard that phrase before!

From the hall Eumorfopoulos took me into rooms in an older part of the house. There I saw twelfth- to thirteenth-century Persian pottery, glass and renaissance enamels, tapestries, particularly the superb Legend of the Handkerchief, medieval stained glass and an example of the synthetic porcelain made for the Medici about 1520, of which only fifty pieces were known to be in existence. 'With a gentle interest,' I noted in my diary, 'he opened his cabinets and explained.' There were mosque lanterns of glass with inscriptions in Kufic calligraphy. To be taken round his collection by so great a connoisseur, frail and in a way mysterious yet tenderly human, was a moving experience for a man in my position. I was still undecided whether to return to Burma or not. The prospect of it filled me with increasing despair.

The room we came to last had contained until a few weeks back the bulk of his Chinese ceramics, which he had sold to the British Museum. I noted: 'There were still several hundred pieces on the shelves, showing to great advantage as they were isolated now. But by this time it was four o'clock.' I had overstayed a luncheon invitation and perhaps overtired my host. I had to drag myself away. Before I left he told me he would take the chair when I read my paper.

It was essential for me to finish my book on Samuel White as soon as I could. If Geoffrey Faber said he would take it, I would have the assurance I required before deciding to leave the Indian Civil Service. I worked with assiduity through the summer. I had not finished the book when I read my paper on the Mergui finds at 8.45 on 9th October 1935 in a room in the London Museum. True to his word, Mr. Eumorfopoulos was in the chair. I had some slides which he had paid for. The lecture lasted fifty-five minutes. There were seventy-five people present, a large number for so specialist a subject. The note in my diary shows me rather smug, though perhaps excusably so: 'It was not a dull paper and was well received. At its close, after a few complimentary remarks by Mr Eumorfopoulos, Mr Hobson, Keeper of the Ceramic Department of the British Museum, and the best known authority and publicist on ceramics in the world, got up and remarked that he accepted my paper as a definite contribution to the knowledge of the subject. A great deal of interest was taken in the fragments, which I displayed on a table. Leading dealers were present, including the Bluetts, Sparks and Norton.'

Unlike most dealers, Mr. Norton made a private collection of Chinese antiquities, which, auctioned after his death, yielded a fortune for his widow.

My diary continues in a self-congratulatory tone, indicative, however, more of intense thankfulness for my good fortune than of conceit: 'I was informed that my paper was one of the best they had had, as it was clear and new. Mr Eumorfopoulos invited me again to lunch, Mrs Walter Sedgwick to tea to meet others of that world. I shall get a ticket for the great Chinese Art exhibition at Burlington House in November.'

Chinese art was much in the air. There were thousands of exhibits at Burlington House brought from China in a battleship and the public crowded in to see them.

I wind up: 'My paper will be printed with illustrations in the Transactions of the O.C. Society, a de luxe publication at 30/– a copy. It has introduced me into the world I so long desired to enter when battling with mosquitoes in the lonely swamps of Burma.'

But, of course, there was no money in all this. It was encouraging but contributed nothing to whether I could afford to clear out of the swamps. That turned on the book. By 9th October, the day I read the paper, I had finished all except the last chapter. Three weeks later I took it to Geoffrey Faber. My diary note of an occasion so momentous for me is: 'I obtained an appointment with Geoffrey Faber, my ancient friend of Rugby and Oxford, and presented myself with the typescript on 28th October. On entering Geoffrey's room I saw him large, kindly and simple as ever. He said he would read the typescript himself and let me know as soon as possible. The book promised to be of interest to his firm, he said encouragingly, though with a touch of caution. It was clear that he would like to publish it if he could. I must wait patiently for a week or so.'

This last sentence gives one pause today, when no publisher makes up his mind about a book under three weeks, for a first book probably six weeks. But I was too unversed in such business to have an idea that promise of an answer in a week or so was very quick.

How unsure I was comes out in the next entry: 'Now that my book is done and my time for return to Burma draws on, I want to see all I can see.' My leave was up in two months. Would the book save me? I was most anxious. I scoured the art galleries in a frantic way. Every moment was precious. In the little time left I must not miss anything. Stanley Spencer had a haunting effect. I saw his now famous 'St. Francis and the Birds', the painting which had just been rejected by the Royal Academy, and, no better than the Academicians, did not appreciate its originality and presence. But curious to relate I did notice in the series of paintings which he was now beginning to exhibit what I termed a corpse-like quality. It was not until twenty-five years later, when writing his biography, that I perceived that a necrophilic perversion was part of his inspiration. It is queer that in 1935 I caught a whiff of this, though such an amateur art critic.

Geoffrey Faber was as good as his word. Ten days after I delivered the book to him I received a message that he would take it and that he thought it 'an exceedingly good one'. 'Bursting with happiness', I note, 'I went to see him that afternoon. He grasped me warmly by the hand and showed on his face how glad he was that he could take it. Frank Morley, one of his directors, then came in. I saw a broad tall man, full of tenderness. He said I had written a remarkable book.' He too had read it during the ten days and his enthusiasm, I was to learn, convinced Faber that the very amateurishness of the writing was proof of some kind of natural talent. We then discussed improvements. A title I had proposed would not do. (Faber thought of the present title, *Siamese White*, some days later in his bath.) My last sentence in the diary entry is: 'My luck has turned.'

I left the room in an emotional state. 'I now have every encouragement to persevere,' I wrote that evening. Yet, was it safe to go at once to the India Office and ask for my proportionate pension? It was safe with £900 a year and such prospects, surely. But could I be certain that there would be enough to educate my children? The family was due shortly for a further increase. Perhaps prospects in Burma were better than they had appeared to me. Changes were coming. The liberalization of the régime seemed increasingly likely. My father, moreover, had warned me not to be rash: 'What a thing to give up the Indian Civil Service, such a position, so certain!' he said. But the old guard was still in power in Rangoon. There was no sure prospect for me there. Nevertheless I still hesitated to ask for pension, despite Faber's and Morley's confidence in me.

I decided, in fact, to go back. It was now the second week in November 1935. If I was really going back I would have to report in Rangoon about the beginning of February 1936 and leave London, my family, everything, about 10th January, my forty-seventh birthday. That I had come to this painful decision can be explained as a momentary lack of confidence in my powers. Since leaving Mergui in October 1934 I had received every sort of encouragement. I had been noticed far beyond my expectations or indeed my understanding, I had written a book which one of the leading publishers of the day had declared remarkable. What was wrong with me that I did not at once seize the opportunity? Lack of confidence, yes, but also the lure of Burma. It was like a siren, that land. In certain moods its dawns, its dusks, its people, its markets, its music rising, compelled me. Had I not done something for its people already, entered into their aspirations, listened to what they told me, encouraged where I could? Would it not be a desertion to leave now, when, as I vaguely guessed, fateful years were approaching? In that mood I went to say farewell to Mr. Eumorfopoulos, of whom I had become fond. My diary has: 'I went feeling more than ever the nearness of my departure, the thousand things I wanted to do but had now no time for, the forlornness of that plunge. He had been ill and I found him in his study, a rug on his knees, very old yet full of a sweetness that was only comparable to the spirit of the lovely objects of oriental art which so long had surrounded him.' We spoke of this and that for a while and I bade him a sorrowful farewell.

Meantime I had written out to the Chief Secretary in Rangoon to ask to what district in Burma I was to be posted on return. I reported that I had written a biography of Samuel White, as there was a rule that a serving Civilian should obtain

George Eumorfopoulos

sanction before he published a book. I received his reply on Christmas Eve. The government had no objection to the proposed publication. As for the posting he said I was to take over charge of the Kyaukpyu district. Kyaukpyu was a port on the Arakan coast, of great charm, a place I had savoured for six months fifteen years before, where I had listened to the wind moaning in the casuarina trees, the sea lapping at the end of the garden, and smelled the scent of the spirit hill on Cheduba island, as recorded later in *Into Hidden Burma*, but it was one of the most out-of-the-way districts, completely cut off from the centre, of small importance, a junior post, and unsuitable for my family as it was malarious for half the year.

I saw in a flash that I could not accept this posting. My head cleared. To return to Burma would be idiotic. There was nothing for me there. Everything that could be done in Burma had been done. It was time for me to be gone. Without further delay I applied to the India Office for proportionate pension. It was granted as the application was in order, and in a fortnight I was free.

The Burma chief secretary may have calculated that his posting of me to Kyaukpyu would oblige me to retire. If I did, what a relief that would be to him! But he did not guess he was doing me a very good turn, perhaps the best turn that any man has ever done me. Had I gone back to duty in Burma I should have found myself overtaken out East by the Second World War, and trapped out there, as all leave was stopped. I should have been separated from my family for many years. It would have been impossible for me, cut off in that way, to have continued writing. Appalling events were close at hand. The Japanese broke in. The British officials had to flee the country, abandoning everything they possessed. In that desperate rout I should have lost my art collections, my papers and my library, and possibly my life. Had I eventually got back to London I should have been about fifty-five years of age, and could hardly then have started on the new career which at forty-seven was opening for me so propitiously. In short, it would have been the ruin of my life. That I did not fall into that pit was due to the Chief Secretary's letter. How strangely do we move back and forth, as destiny unwinds its web.

I had packed all my boxes and now unpacked them. Word was sent to the customs officer in Mergui to hand over the packing cases there, which he had been faithfully looking after for over a year, to Thomas Cook & Son to ship to London. He did so and they arrived in due course. Nothing was broken except two fifteenth-century Ming blue and white dishes, which I had bought in a Rangoon shop in 1928 for £6 the pair. These two dishes were a Ming variety which during the last five years has rushed up in value. Had I known when I unpacked them finally in London that thirty years later they would, if unbroken, have been worth as much as a Vlaminck or an Utrillo, it would have been a shock to find them in pieces. As it was, the loss of a matter of £6 was trifling considering the stupid risks to which I had left the cases exposed.

Siamese White, accepted on 7th November 1935, was published 20th February 1936. At that date a book could be got through the press in three months and a half. How it was received is the subject of the next chapter.

2

Starting a new career

WHEN *Siamese White* came out on 20th February 1936 I had been drawing my pension for just over a month. Its figure of £900 a year was rather less than my leave pay had been. Having no savings I had barely enough for the expense of setting up house in England; the Adelaide Road address was only lodgings. I would require a lump sum to carry me over the period of transition and I hoped the book would provide some of it. But I had no experience, nothing to guide me. It might earn very little. Most books don't earn much. Faber & Faber did not think it safe to give me more than an advance of £50 against future royalties. In short, I awaited publication day without more than a vague idea of probabilities.

Then suddenly everything went at a gallop. The day after publication the book was reviewed in the *Times Literary Supplement* and given a whole half page as if a volume of importance. Three days later Basil de Selincourt, the *Observer*'s main literary critic, gave it two columns of praise. When I wrote and thanked him he replied on a postcard: 'It is a topping book.' This set the ball rolling fast. The same week the *Evening Standard* splashed it in a full page and the *Illustrated London News* made it their choice for the week. The Book Society now joined in the enthusiasm and entered it on their 'recommended' list. At this stage the film companies began to make offers. Best of all it attracted the attention of David Garnett, one of the most influential members of the Bloomsbury set, for he had been an intimate friend of Lytton Strachey's. His admiration for *Siamese*

White was capital, far more important than I realized at the time. He belonged to the most exclusive group in English letters, well known for its acerbity. Authors mostly got a slap, at best a patronizing pat. But apparently in this case he was carried away.

That the films were interested now became generally known. On 6th March, just a fortnight after publication, I got a letter from David Garnett. He said: 'I think *Siamese White* would be a magnificent subject for a film. I know several people in the film world and will try to have the attention of a film magnate directed to it. I wonder whether you would consider collaboration in the preparation of a script.' And he goes on to say he would like to come to some arrangement. 'There is a lot of money, I believe, in these things.' For David Garnett, a famous literary personality, to want to collaborate with a person like myself who had suddenly arrived on the scene with only an Indian Civil Service background—a black mark on the whole— was an extraordinary compliment. But so innocent was I that I took it all as a matter of course. It seemed good luck, no more. As I had never had good luck before, I had nothing to measure it by; I did not realize that so much notice for a first book was extremely rare. I accepted it as a hungry man accepts a good helping and looks out for a second.

A second was coming. The very day I received David Garnett's letter, Geoffrey Faber wrote to say that a film company had offered £1,750 down for the rights of *Siamese White* with an advance fee of £250 for assistance with the film script. Faber closed with the offer at once. 'America might have offered more,' he wrote, 'but it is better to take a good offer cash down in England.' Under his contract with me, he was entitled to get 25 per cent of any film offer, but prompted by his good heart he reduced it to 17½ per cent, thereby making me a present of about £150. What happened afterwards about David Garnett's offer I do not remember. Anyhow, no film was produced. The film company paid up but did not go on with it. Film companies at this time were very flush. A shot with a thousand or two was thought a legitimate gamble. At first they believed *Siamese White* would make a fortune like *The Mutiny on the Bounty*. They changed their minds and made the fortune with something else.

At the moment, however, I was more than a thousand and a half to the good. My diary has: 'This completely solves the problem of how I am going to live on my pension. The simultaneous publication of so many good reviews has made the book. At one stroke I have got the reputation of a writer. It is all too good to be true.' Feeling I ought to follow up my success at once, I tried to think of a fresh subject. And noted: 'I must remain calm, not expect too much and work hard,' adding, 'and make myself as agreeable as possible'. This was written on 10th March 1936. By 11th June 1936 I record that I had written 80,000 words of a new book. *Siamese White* by that time had reached a second printing.

Siamese White's reception in Burma was mixed. The then Governor, unlike Sir Harcourt Butler in the twenties, did not write to congratulate me. The Secretaries to the government were mum. The only bookshop in Rangoon, though it stocked the book, gave out that as no one could suppose I had written it, a brother of mine, who had published a book or two, must have done it. In the Rangoon clubs, on the contrary, it was conceded I had done it, but that it was a dirty piece of work, just the sort of thing I would do, running down an Englishman. True, White was undeniably a bit disreputable and lived nearly two hundred years back, but I should have 'kept my mouth shut and not given the natives ammunition for their anti-British propaganda'. My friends out there stood up for me; English, Burmese, Indians and Chinese wrote saying how glad they were. B. C. Rake, recently retired from the position of deputy Inspector General of Police, sent a letter saying he was 'awfully pleased, particularly as it was a success over the Burma government, who had sent me to Mergui to smother me'. Another friend, Frank Fearnley-Whittingstall, who had been Private Secretary to Sir Harcourt Butler when he was Governor, gave a party in London to celebrate the occasion, to which Sir Harcourt came.

These good wishes from Burma, though they meant a lot to me, meant nothing in London, where the critics and the public had led the way in praising the book. In the end, its various editions, with Penguin, Albatross and other paperbacks, have sold about 200,000 copies and it is still selling. But it has never been filmed, though later on more film companies took options. Moreover, no American publisher has ever brought an edition out, in spite of it being the sort of adventure story supposedly the rage over there. I was told it was not written in the popular style required. Being a real historical biography, with everything taken from the original documents and without any invented conversations, was against it.

So much for my first step as an author. But could I keep it up? I had to, somehow. I have mentioned how I got to work at once on another book. The first thing, however, was to set up house. I bought furniture in the Campden Hill second-hand shops and in Earls Court Road, choosing if I could Georgian and early Victorian pieces, which at that date, and bought in such a modest neighbourhood, were very cheap. The Caledonian market nearby was also a source. I bought there for £5 a large picture of dragon dogs by Shen Ch'uan, whose sobriquet was Nam-p'ing (Southern Duckweed). Later on Arthur Waley confirmed it was indeed by that eighteenth-century master. In the same market I came on Hiroshige's 'Monkey Bridge' (one of his most celebrated prints) lying on the cobblestones with a brick holding it down, and bought it for two and six.

The question was where to live, in London or out of it; if the latter, where? During the past year I had made the acquaintance of Staite Murray, the potter. Eumorfopoulos held a high opinion of him as an artist. He had some of his pots in the study off the hall as I noticed on my first visit and often spoke of him to me. I asked to be introduced. When this was arranged, I discovered him to be an artist who drew his inspiration from oriental thought. He liked to think that his pots had a Taoist import. Bernard Leach, his only rival at this time, leant more towards the Zen of Japan. These two men were the best studio potters of the thirties, though they did not admire each other's work. Staite Murray's public support was the greater and he was able to charge more. One of his bowls was at this time placed on exhibition in the

Victoria & Albert as the 'masterpiece of the month'. In my first conversation with him, he thought, since I had lived in Burma, I was bound to understand his art better than did the run of London critics. Among them he was held little more than a craftsman, he complained, though he looked on himself as an artist who had chosen pots as his vehicle of expression. Speaking rather like a lecturer he pronounced the following *obita dicta*. 'I have worked for thirty years but the public does not understand me. The appreciation of potting is the most difficult of the connoisseurships. There are high singing pots full of poetry and the open air, others are dark with a writhing sensuality, others stout as a wall or a turret weathered by age. A great pot is a magical object. Power flows from it, sometimes beneficent, sometimes sinister. It is a synthesis of earth, air, water and fire. I do not claim to make my pots. On the wheel the clay as it revolves seems to rise up into its predestined shape.'

As I listened to him pouring out these notions he became yet more convinced that I was a congenial spirit and asked me to stay a weekend at his studio at Bray, a couple of miles from Maidenhead. This I did; his pottery aesthetic was intriguing and I greatly admired his work, though more for its plain qualities of colour and shape than for the mystical qualities he attributed to it. While at Bray I told him I wanted to rent a house out of London. Could he recommend some locality? Why not Maidenhead? he asked. It would be a great pleasure to have me near him. I could write a book on his art, explain him to the world and advance the art of potting in England.

It was this that prompted me to suggest to my family that we should choose Maidenhead. It was, moreover, situated on one of the most beautiful reaches of the Thames and within an hour's motor run of London. A house was found. We moved down in the spring of 1936 about a month after the publication of *Siamese White*.

On further acquaintance with Staite Murray I found his ideas about pots too fanciful to treat seriously. Anxious for me to write a book about him, more especially since the success of my book on Samuel White, he continued to dilate upon the subject and placed at my disposal papers and notes of his own. While my admiration for his pots was undiminished—I have to this day a dozen of them in my house—I saw that I could not conscientiously endorse the interpretations which he gave to them, and to his chagrin abandoned the book idea. He had a hortatory style of talking, which enabled him to collect round him a body of devotees in the manner of an oriental sage, but his education, reading and, indeed, intellect, were not on a level with his artistic gifts. His work was delightful, his talk tedious. He liked to shoot off mots which impressed his admirers. Thus, I heard him correct a visitor who, anxious to show himself appreciative, declared that his pots were like men: 'No, no, men are like my pots.' I also came upon him one day in the garden with a hammer in his hand among a number of pots in pieces. He was in the act of breaking up another one, which seemed to me of excellent quality. 'Stop, stop!' said I, quite taken aback. 'It's got to be broken,' said he. 'What's wrong with it?' I pleaded. 'An evil spirit has taken possession of it,' he replied, and struck it a blow that smashed it in two. I carried away the largest half, which I have to this day, though he warned me it was dangerous to have anything to do with it.

In spite of such extravagances, which, though they had an endearing quality, were clearly nonsense and could in no way be advanced as proof of his artistic talent, I was fond of him, often saw him, and tried when possible to be useful to him.

During the summer and autumn of this, my first year, at Maidenhead, I worked hard and finished the new book which I hoped Fabers would accept. This was submitted on 7th September and came out in April 1937, quick work again, though it seemed slow to me for Geoffrey Faber had spoiled me. I find a note dated 25th October 1936 to the effect that I rang him up impatiently, complaining about the delay in getting a decision. 'I have only had time to read half the book so far,' he explained. However, before Christmas he accepted it, in spite of being, as he wrote, behind with other books he had to read. It was he who invented the title, *She was a Queen*.

It is a risky thing to follow up a lucky book like *Siamese White*.

You are bound to get critics who compare the first to the detriment of the second. But my luck held. *Siamese White* was made by David Garnett, *She was a Queen* by James Agate. The book suited his taste and he let himself go in the *Daily Express*. Howard Spring joined in. Three thousand copies of the English edition were sold and it was translated into German, Norwegian, Swedish and French.

I came on its subject after reading my old friend Gordon Luce's masterly translation of the *Glass Palace Chronicle*, a work of mingled folklore, legend and history of great charm, compiled by Burmese scholars in 1829 at the instance of the King of Ava. Combined with twenty years' acquaintance with rural Burma, it enabled me to create a Burmese atmosphere. Therein lay what merit my book possessed. It was a dream of old Burma as the Burmese themselves imagined it before modern scholarship dissipated that dream. Though Gordon Luce liked my book for literary reasons, he feared it might give currency to incorrect historical notions, a natural reaction for a man who for many years had been trying to sort out from the documents the bare truth. He has devoted his life to elucidating the middle period of Burmese history, a task which has involved him in researches among not only Burmese sources but Mon and Chinese. His task is completed, I understand, and his book is about to appear. That he can have retained any regard for *She was a Queen* is hardly to be supposed, a book dashed off in a few months. When he reflects, however, that it is all his fault because he provided the inspiration by translating so richly the *Glass Palace Chronicle*, it may be that he relents. If he remains inflexible, it suffices that he also remains, as I believe, attached to me.

While waiting with rude impatience for Geoffrey Faber to make up his mind about *She was a Queen*, I received on 7th October 1936 a letter from a Mr. Twentyman, a senior Treasury official, who was head of a so-called clearing office concerned with the financing of foreign trade in England. He required a colleague and had been advised by the India Office that I would be suitable. Why the India Office, presumably in touch with the powers in Rangoon, recommended me, is a mystery. I have in my diary:

'Though without any intention at present of seeking a job, for I must try out my fate as a writer, I decided to call on Mr Twenty-man.' Supposing Fabers declined *She was a Queen* it might be as well to have something to fall back on.

When ushered into his presence I found someone very unlike the popular conception of a Treasury official. 'He had a goatee beard, large eyes and his hair was brushed back into a mane of yellowish grey colour. He looked like Conrad.' In a *de haut en bas* manner he explained what the appointment involved. It was whole-time, arduous and responsible. The holder would have a large staff. One might often not get away before 7 p.m. Some acquaintance with the theory of foreign exchange would be useful. The salary would be £800 a year (which added to my pension of £900 would give a comfortable income). But the job was so utterly unsuitable for me that Mr. Twentyman noticed my waning interest and hinted that perhaps I did not care for the idea. I replied that I was in an unusual position, having published that year a book which had met with great success. Had he by any chance heard of *Siamese White*?

'What!' he exclaimed. 'Are you the author of *Siamese White*? That is a lovely book. I am delighted to see you!' When he said that I felt a warm blush right into my hair. He continued with animation: 'Oh you must not think of wasting your time in an office! Go on with your writing.'

Hardly out of the clutches of Rangoon officialdom, it was an ironic twist to be thought by a senior London official too good for a Foreign Office appointment that doubled my pay. By this time Mr. Twentyman and I were on excellent terms. I thanked him warmly for his good opinion and encouraging advice. It was time to leave and I got up. We shook hands very cordially. 'You know, I myself have always longed to write,' he said with a melancholy look on his Conrad visage.

This diverting interview took place, as stated, on 7th October 1936, while Faber was still considering *She was a Queen*. When he made up his mind in December to publish it I was thankful for having found the resolution to accept Mr. Twentyman's advice and go on trying my luck as an author rather than surrender to the lure of a safe £800 a year. The book came out in April 1937 and had the encouraging reception I have recounted.

I was in such a hurry to get on that in May I began a new book, later entitled *Trials in Burma*. By the end of the summer it was finished. I was satisfied with the way I had managed a very delicate subject and felt that it connected me with Burma more closely than had *She was a Queen*. I viewed it as my contribution to the cause of Burma. It was accepted by Faber at the end of September, who paid an advance of £150. This was more than double what he paid for *She was a Queen* which was only £60 in spite of the success of *Siamese White*. But the success of both these two books was more a *succès d'estime* than a sales success. That kind of success pays best in the end, but meanwhile you can't live on it. Faber was right to be cautious until the esteem matured into cash.

A subject for another book unexpectedly came up. In August 1937 Philip Fogarty, the brother-in-law of Bernard Swithinbank, came down to see me at Maidenhead. I had known him well since 1930–1 when he backed me up in the controversial cases I tried as magistrate in Rangoon, and which had startled the officials whose opinions dominated the government. Since then he had become Commissioner of the Shan States, a delightful appointment. As such he represented the Crown in the Shan States, an appanage of Burma where the hereditary princes still lived in state and ruled as feudatories under a general British supervision. The climate of the States was good, the Princes and their families celebrated for their charm. 'Come out and stay with me,' said Fogarty as he sat in the drawing-room at Maidenhead. 'I'll take you on a tour of the courts, introduce you all round. In a month or so you'll have the material for an unusual travel book. No one knows a thing about the Shans here. You really must come.' He was most enthusiastic. I replied that if Faber would advance money for the book I would come.

After Fogarty left it crossed my mind that the tour would not please the Old Guard in Burma. They had been so relieved when I left the country for good. Now I would be popping up again, a figure, too, of more consequence after the good reception I had been given by learned and literary London. But as Fogarty was inviting me, a Civilian in one of the top appointments, whose brother-in-law, Bernard Swithinbank, was now Commissioner of Pegut, an appointment which gave him administrative charge of the capital, Rangoon, surely the Old Guard's feelings did not matter. I could not be censured for coming out to write a travel book on the Shan States. I went to work to get Geoffrey Faber and his directors to agree.

I kept Fogarty informed, after he had returned to his duties, about the way things were shaping. But he did not answer my letters. By the end of October 1937 Faber agreed to advance £200, fifty pounds more than his advance for *Trials in Burma*, due for publication in April 1938. An American publisher put up another hundred. On getting these assurances I booked a passage by P. & O. for 1st January 1938, tourist class return at £90. That left me £160 to cover other expenses of the tour and give me a profit on the book, not a large sum. But I was so keen on the idea of revisiting Burma after an absence of three years and touring in congenial company the Shan plateau, of which I had no previous experience, that I did not look too closely into the business side. What worried me was that I had received no word from Fogarty. Did his silence indicate that he no longer expected me? Could it be that he regretted having invited me and hoped his silence would be hint enough to keep off? It was hard to say. I sought reassurance by writing to his wife, Swithinbank's sister, who was in England, and received a reply that she had no reason to think her husband had changed his mind, and attributed his silence to press of work. Anyhow, it was too late to cancel my plans, now that contracts had been signed in England and America for a Shan travel book. I wrote out to tell Fogarty I was starting on 1st January 1938 and would be with him before the end of that month.

It now occurred to me for the first time as probable that Fogarty had got nervous in case the government blamed him for having invited me. As there was no turning back and I had to go, I decided to seek help elsewhere and wrote to Noel Whiting, an old friend who lived in Rangoon and was well acquainted with the Shan lords, to ask whether he could motor me round, if the other arrangement fell through. He let me know at once that he would be delighted to do so, and would meet me on the wharf at Rangoon. With this assurance in my pocket I set sail.

Sure enough on the steamer coming alongside, there was Noel Whiting waiting, as loyal a friend as I have ever met in my life. It was a great relief. Fogarty had sent nobody to meet me nor any message. I wired up to say I had arrived, was staying a day or so with Whiting in Rangoon, and would then be driven up by him to Taung-gyi, the headquarters of the Shan administration, over three hundred miles away to the north.

On our getting to Taung-gyi, Fogarty received me in a cordial manner and no reference at the moment was made to his disconcerting silence. The explanation, as I afterwards gathered from Whiting, was not dissimilar to what I had surmised. On reflection he had regretted having asked me to come out because he was afraid what the government would say. But as an old friend, who had a warm regard for me, he shrank from writing to say the invitation was off, trusting that I would divine from his neglecting to answer my letters the embarrassing situation in which he found himself. Now that I was at his door he could not bear to let Whiting take me round. Indeed, he was cold to him, as to an intruder, who had schemed to tempt me away from him. For he was much taken with the prospect of conducting an author round his domain to write a book in which he was sure to figure. Besides that, he was an old friend and was certain he would enjoy my companionship.

This was all very ludicrous but it did show that the Burma executive had a sort of horror of me, which was a compliment. I had not been accused of any breach of the rules, because I had never broken any rules. But in a way hard to specify I was alarming. It was impossible to tell what I might do next. As soon as they heard that I had reached the Shan States they wired to Fogarty directing him to report why I had come. He replied that my sole object was to write a travel book. This plain truth stumped them. It could not be gainsaid, but they remained suspicious.

The tour was extremely pleasant and resulted in my book *Lords of the Sunset*. After the tour I stayed a few days with Bernard Swithinbank in Rangoon. When it was known I was there some Burmese notabilities got up a dinner for me. Swithinbank was asked, but even he, a man not easily intimidated, thought it prudent to decline the invitation, though not afraid to put me up. It was to this atmosphere that the first copies of *Trials in Burma*, published in London on 2nd April, arrived in Rangoon. As the book was in a few places uncomplimentary to the very people with whom Fogarty and even Swithinbank felt they had to be circumspect, I began to feel a trifle apprehensive myself and to avoid unpleasantness thought it better to leave and so took the next boat home.

Back in England, however, I found *Trials in Burma* the book of the month. It had aroused the interest of such reviewers as Harold Nicolson and Robert Lynd. My tone amused, the book was called a comedy. J. K. Stanford, a former Burma Civilian and a noted author of books on sport, said in a letter to me: 'I had the satisfaction of telling Cunliffe about *Trials* and watching him going more and more purple in the face. He could sit for a portrait of Jorrocks now.' Mr. Justice Cunliffe, late of the Rangoon High Court, cut a poor figure in a certain passage. He consulted his lawyers, I was told, but learned that he had no chance of winning a libel suit. He has not been heard of since, except for a miniscule obituary in *The Times*. Lady Rhondda, proprietor and editor of *Time and Tide*, wrote asking me to become a regular contributor to her paper, particularly to her feature, 'Notes on the Way', a weekly commentary on current affairs. Later she also made me the paper's art critic.

When one considers that the subject of *Trials in Burma* was concerned in the main with cases tried seven years before in a magistrate's court in Rangoon, a place few people in England had heard of, it is astonishing that the British public should have found it readable.

While basking in the warmth of public smiles I wrote *Lords of the Sunset*, the account of my Shan tour, and handed it to Geoffrey Faber in July 1938. Somehow or other he managed to publish it in October, a feat the wonder of which I did not fully appreciate, as he had dreadfully spoiled me. My Christmas card that year was a photo of the Shan girl called Lady Laughing Water. Even Swithinbank unbent when he got it and wrote on 8th January 1939: 'I have been in love with that lady since my first reading (of several) of *Lords of the Sunset*.' The book was dedicated to Philip Fogarty who, adds Swithinbank, 'sends his love'. Both of these eminent Civilians were delighted with it and, no longer nervous at my being in Burma, were able wholeheartedly to send me their affection. The letters from the Shan princesses were effusive. Some of them have remained correspondents to this day.

Delightful though I found the Shans and their country, I suffered while there an attack of claustrophobia, a variety of home sickness, though I was in the Shan States for under two months. This attack, very acute while it lasted, as I record in my book, warned me never again to visit Burma or indeed any place where I was cut off from London. Since that time I have travelled no farther than Naples, and then was safeguarded by having my daughter with me.

Lords of the Sunset was swallowed by the critics with a gulp of pleasure. A fresh lot of influential reviewers flattered me, people like Malcolm Muggeridge, then hardly started on his spiral to celebrity, and V. S. Pritchett, already much admired for his stories, which have such a tonic bite. The Swedes paid for a translation. In a letter dated 9th December 1938 Sir Joseph Maung Gyi, who had acted as Governor of Burma in 1931, wrote urging me to make one more visit to his country. He told me that 'the pagoda on a little island opposite Mergui town is now known as Collis Paya'. This struck me as the most agreeable compliment ever paid to me.

The profit in cash made by the book was small, about £100 after deduction of expenses. It was published at an ominous moment. With a public watching in apprehension the drift towards a Second World War, the autumn of 1938 was the wrong moment to bring out a book on an Asian arcadia. Fabers did not print a second impression after the first one of 2,000 copies was exhausted, because they were not sure they could sell it, even though the book's reception in the press had been so encouraging. Being myself foolishly optimistic and ready to believe that a *modus vivendi* could be arranged with Hitler, I did not perceive that we had to do with a murderous fanatic. My luck so far had been marvellous. But if Europe was going to be turned upside down, what would be the lot of a writer whose subject was the oriental phantasmagoria? I did not worry and without ado started away on a work of fiction. This was handed in to Geoffrey Faber at the end of May 1939. On 28th June I received a letter from him seeking to dissuade me from having it published. 'I would not be serving your interests faithfully if I concealed my honest view. So here goes—and may you forgive me!' His main criticism was that in spite of excellent passages the plot had a clumsy doctored look. 'I am not infallible. But I think, nevertheless, that I am right and that you would be wise to suppress this book.' But he wound up by saying that should I refuse to do so, 'we would publish, rather than let you go'.

One can hardly imagine a more tender letter. His view, of course, was upsetting, but on reflection I felt he was right. The book *was* inferior to its four predecessors. My difficulty was, however, that I could not afford to suppress it. If I did, I should have little or nothing with which to supplement my pension until I had written something else. Perhaps it was not quite as bad as he made out. It had good bits, I thought. Anyhow, I was prepared to take the risk to my reputation and I pressed him to publish. This he did in October 1939, making me an advance of £75. It came out under the title of *Sanda Mala*. As the Second World War had just begun, everyone was in a state of nerves. Geoffrey himself took so gloomy a view of his own affairs that he spoke to me of his despair at the prospect of seeing his business, which he had worked up from nothing, go to ruin.

But again my luck held. I had placed *Sanda Mala* in the hands of a literary agent, the well-known Mr. A. D. Peters. Soon after its publication he rang me up and with admirable sang-froid announced that he had sold it to an American film company for fifteen thousand dollars. That was less in sterling than it is today, but incalculably more in purchasing power. An American edition

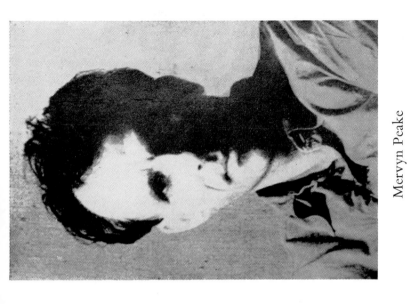

Mervyn Peake

Sir George Grierson, O.M.

also was shortly announced. In a stroke I was delivered from financial worries. A bad reception from the London reviewers might have damped my good spirits. But I did not get a bad reception. No one wrote with such candid sorrow as did Geoffrey Faber. The clapping was not so loud as in the case of my previous books, but it made a decent reverberation. Faber wrote saying that evidently my judgment on my own work was better than his, a charming admission. *Sanda Mala* was not made into a film, but I was beginning to learn that sale or rights by no means guaranteed production. My payment turned out pure charity on the part of the company. It is an error to declare that film magnates are not patrons of literature. Their awards far exceed those given by societies professing to help struggling authors.

Though as it happened the decision to get Faber to publish *Sanda Mala* did me well in a financial way, I feel now that he was right about the book's literary failings. Today I think no better of it than he did in 1938.

3

I begin writing on China

THE DECLARATION OF WAR against Germany on 3rd September 1939 was no surprise. But one had hoped against hope that war would be avoided. We had passed a wretched August listening to the news, which fluctuated, now better, now more menacing. When the declaration came on the 3rd I noted: 'It cleared the air and everyone felt much more cheerful.' I was fifty years of age. I conceived, however, that I should offer my services in some capacity and give up writing while the war lasted. So on 4th September I went up to London by an early train to make inquiries. I have in my diary: 'At Paddington there was a great crowd of people leaving in packed trains. (A bombing raid was expected any moment.) Outside it was strangely still, unlike a Sunday, for the shops were open but like Sunday as there was little traffic and few pedestrians.' I took a bus to Russell Square and went into No. 24 to see Faber, as that seemed the first thing to do. He had not come up from the country. Another director saw me and said that 'the firm would continue business till the office was untenable'. As mentioned in the last chapter *Sanda Mala* came out a month after the declaration of war, so that I had as yet no knowledge of how the book would go and that fifteen thousand dollars was in the offing. But from what the director said it seemed I could count on the publication at least.

I next went to see my agent, Peters. He told me that if I wanted to offer my services, I should apply to the Ministry of Information for a job. He knew them there and could recommend me as an expert on eastern affairs. A paid job of some kind was what I needed to supplement my pension if it should prove impossible to go on writing.

From Peters I went on to the office of *Time & Tide* and had a cup of coffee and a talk with Lady Rhondda's secretary, Miss Gimingham. Did she think they could continue to produce *Time & Tide*? I had already begun to contribute articles and reviews of books. One was paid little, but it added up with luck to perhaps £70 a year. She could not say whether they would be able to continue publication. Lady Rhondda hoped to do so, but no one could tell what the future held in store. She asked me whether they could count on me and I assured her they could.

My next call was at the India Office. I went to the room of the Secretary of State's adviser on Burma affairs. He was able to let me know that it was not proposed to recall retired Civilians to duty in Burma, a piece of news which I was most relieved to hear, as a rumour to the contrary had alarmed me. I was informed too that the India Office was making no appointments in England and if I wanted to do war work, paid or unpaid, I should apply to the Ministry of Labour for registration, though as I was over fifty it was not likely that I would be offered anything.

My diary has: 'This cleared the air a good deal. I begin to see how I stand. A job is unlikely. But provided I can summon the necessary calm, I will continue to write. The chief anxiety is to make a pension, insufficient without supplement, suffice if publication becomes impossible.'

I started back for Maidenhead, walking to Paddington via the Marble Arch. In St. James's the art shops had little in the windows, which were protected from blast by adhesive tape or shuttered. This made me reflect on my own art collection. 'Near the Arch was a solitary speaker with a fair crowd. He was speaking of biblical prophecy and the Second Coming.' When I got home I began packing the best pieces of my Chinese porcelain collection in case a bomb came down near the house.

By 7th September I was calmer and able to 'concentrate my mind again on literary projects'. My novel *Sanda Mala* was due for publication on 19th October since Faber had decided to carry on as before. I had, while awaiting his decision, started a further fictional narrative and now continued its composition. He was told of this new book. His preference would have been for me to leave fiction and even to abandon the subject of Burma. 'Why not try Ireland, your own native land?' he wrote. But in October–November after *Sanda Mala*'s unlooked for success he let me alone to go my own way. The new novel, if it could be so called, had a connection with the war, for in a way it had to do with what the Japanese might attempt should they overrun China, which already appeared possible. As far back as 1934, when I was in Mergui, it was currently rumoured in the bazaar that one day the Japanese would enter Burma in that region. They were vaguely seen as the deliverers foretold in the old prophecy I had heard in 1921 when Deputy Commissioner of Kyaukpyu that Burma would regain its independence through the actions of a person or persons coming in from the outside. There were some Japanese residents in Mergui in my day. The town's photographer was of that nation as was one of the pearl divers, the man who, as I have recorded in my *Into Hidden Burma*, fished up from the depths of the sea opposite my house a Chinese celadon dish, which Sir Percival David later assured me one day in London I was right in dating twelfth or thirteenth century. When my people, hearing of his find, asked the diver to sell me the dish, he showed at first some reluctance, as he declared his intention of presenting it to the Emperor of Japan. But cash down persuaded him. He and the photographer, better educated and more percipient than men of the sort usually are, were thought to be Japanese secret agents, the one taking soundings off the coast and the other photos of the land. In fact, the Japanese did enter Burma in January 1942 in that region after crossing the Malay Peninsula at a spot called Kra pass, east of Victoria Point, the southernmost townlet in my jurisdiction. I was well acquainted with the Kra pass and had advised the government that a Japanese thrust over it would turn the fortress of Singapore.

With these memories of 1934 in mind I invented a plot for my new novel some months before the declaration of war and two years before the Japanese launched their offensive westwards after Pearl Harbor. I finished the book by the end of 1939. On the face of it the story seemed about a British secret agent sent to investigate alleged Japanese preparations to cut the Malay Peninsula by digging a canal at Kra, its narrowest point. Faber accepted it as a thriller which would sell at a time when the question of the impregnability of Singapore, the bastion of the Indian Empire, was a subject of discussion. But my intention had not been to write a thriller, a feat of which anyhow I was incapable. The book was a comedy, a sort of gambol on my part among the fancies and beliefs of Burmese villagers in a remote spot, the Kra pass. I adored these fancies, Buddhistic, metaphysical, magical, supernatural. It gave me immense pleasure to frisk among them, amused and happy, indeed fondly moved by the beauty of the *mise en scène*. Alchemy, astrology, miracles, had something so delightfully human behind their dreaming. Everything was Nothing, Nothing was Everything and Everywhere was Otherwhere. How delicious to wallow in a warm sea of Non-Sense!

Geoffrey and his coadjutors decided to put out this farce as a thriller and it was published under the title of *The Dark Door*, words which I had culled from an ancient Sanscrit canticle that began: 'The Dark Door is deep and solitary, its doctrine is unique and expressed in subtle words.' The date of publication in May 1940 coincided almost exactly with the German in-rush and the fall of Paris, a moment of such consternation that valuables went for nothing in the auction rooms. I looked into Sotheby's the day Paris fell because part of George Eumorfopoulos's collection was for sale. (He had died some months before.) The principal items were his modern sculptures, the Mestrovics, Epsteins, Skeapings, Gills, etc. which I had admired in his house. It was the moment of Churchill's speech: 'We will fight on the beaches.' Invasion seemed only a few days distant. No one wanted to encumber himself with stone or bronze. He wanted what he could carry as he fled. That dreadful day you could buy an Epstein for ten or fifteen pounds. As I remember, the only piece of his which topped twenty was the head of a smiling child.

That was the unpropitious date when *The Dark Door* appeared on the bookstalls, a gallopade through the Mahayanist metaphysic of Nothing, a roaring farce on the theory of non-Such. Who could spare a moment for such a book when the foundations of Britain were tottering? But as a war thriller, what about that? No, the critics as they crouched listening for the tramp of Hitler's legions, could not accept it as that. *The Times Literary Supplement*, however, allowed it to be amusing; the *Observer* was at a loss; the *Spectator* admitted that it had 'a curious perfume and most melodious twang'; Richard Church in *John O'London's* thought it extraordinary but could not make head or tail of it. The magazine, *Buddhism in England*, though perceiving that a sense of fun pervaded it, compared me to an impish Zen master, who treats his disciples to paradoxes the better to suggest the profundities of his doctrines. This was a compliment coming from that source but it was not true. My fun was not used to propagate Buddhism. I had given a hint to Faber by telling him that the manner of my text was comparable to a police report on, say, the coming to Bethlehem of the Three Kings. The only person to my knowledge who got the book right was Bernard Swithinbank. I sent him a copy to Burma and on 20th May he wrote to thank me from an address in Malaya where he was spending some leave, for at the outbreak of war no home leave was sanctioned. Officials were prisoners for the duration, as I had been during the four years of the First World War, and would have been again had I not got out in 1934.

The letter ran: 'I was proud to receive your book; I could not say this of *Sanda Mala* which though I did not dislike I could not take seriously: this book I thoroughly enjoyed.

'This was not the first or the second of your books to show the grim pleasure you take in the mumbo-jumbo which is so important to Burmese minds. Never before have you been so completely successful in the *pince-sans-rire* method. I can appreciate this although I hate the thing itself, and wish to forget about it, except when the education of my youth tells, and I wish to *écraser l'infâme*. (You had the same sort of education, why the difference? I suppose to be satisfied with Voltaire is a sign of my arrested spiritual development; I won't speculate on your spiritual state!)

'The book has given me great pleasure, all the more because you sent it.'

Bernard Swithinbank had literary insight of the first order. His mental equipment surpassed that of the newspaper critics who reviewed the book. His letter meant everything to me. I understood for the first time that my style or tone was naturally *pince-sans-rire*. I was able to use it in the best of my future books, such as *The Great Within*, though sometimes I was so bemused by the beauty of the oriental background as almost to credit its reality.

The Dark Door's only chance as a seller was that the thriller public would be silly enough to buy it. That mistake they did not make. The public composed of people like Swithinbank was put off by the publisher's suggestion that it was a thriller, except for a number so small as to be insufficient to keep the book alive. It just repaid the small advance and then disappeared and has never been heard of since. Yet it is a book which of all my books dealing with Burma I like best and often reread, never with tedium. But anyone curious to read it will find it hard to get hold of; the London Library even has no copy. Such is the sad situation of my favourite child, until Faber & Faber bring out a new edition, which I am sure will not happen in my lifetime. If Bernard Swithinbank were alive I could get him to push it in a Voltairean letter, but alas! he died in the forties.

Having by 1940 published six books with a Burma theme since I started writing in 1935, I began to see the force of Geoffrey Faber's comment that it was time to try my hand on a fresh subject. China had been attracting me for some time; my collection of Chinese antiquities had partially opened the door. I had never been there, though I had lived adjacent and even crossed the frontier into Yunnan when on my tour of the Shan States, an incursion, however, of less than a mile. After coming to London in 1935, before I had published anything, I called on Arthur Waley. The sixth volume was out of his celebrated translation of the Lady Mursaki's *Tale of Genji*, the masterpiece of Japanese eleventh-century literature. I had also bought and admired his translations from the Chinese poets. I found him in the British Museum's Department of Prints where till 1929 he had worked. Gordon Luce, an old friend of his, gave me the introduction, though as Arthur Waley and I had been contemporaries at Rugby School thirty years previously we were vaguely known to each other. A classical scholar at the top of the school, while I had nothing to show for myself except a certain facility in writing school essays, we had hardly spoken to each other. But now in 1935 when I presented myself with Luce's letter he was agreeably civil. Exactly my age, his hair was dark, his eyes large, his expression distinguished. I said I wanted to read more about China. Could he advise me how to start? He replied: 'Read Giles's Chinese Biographical Dictionary.' That concluded his advice. It was as if he considered my question naïve, as indeed it was. Like Naaman, the Syrian, when told by Elisha to go and wash in the Jordan, I felt he might have been a little more forthcoming. But like Elisha he had said all that was necessary. I immediately got out Giles's biographical dictionary and found it as good or better than Aubrey's *Brief Lives*. I have continued to dip into it ever since. Many of the little biographies are extremely vivid, particularly the one about the indigent poet Chia Tao (A.D. 777–841) which has a literary slant just right for this context. The outstanding event in Chia Tao's life was his meeting with Han Yü, so celebrated a writer that it was customary to wash the hands in rose water before opening one of his books. Chia Tao was in the habit of composing his verses as he walked the streets of the capital. One day, uncertain whether to use the word push or knock in a certain passage, he was going through the motions of pushing and knocking to get the feel of the words, and did not look where he was going. As chance would have it, he knocked down one of the bearers of the sedan chair in which Han Yü was being carried. Besides his standing as a man of letters, Han Yü was officially high up for he was Viceroy of the Metropolitan Province; in those days literature was better rewarded than now. To irritate such a personage by upsetting his sedan was the last thing that Chia Tao intended. His apologies were profuse and he explained the circumstances: he had been trying out a line of verse. As soon as Han

Yü understood that it was all a matter of prosody, the displeasure he had felt evaporated. He invited Chia Tao to sit with him in the sedan and discuss the problem as they were carried along. On getting home he offered the starveling poet a post in his household.

Though not so dramatic, my meeting with Arthur Waley was not wholly dissimilar. It was as happy a rencounter as Chia Tao's with Han Yü. I became Waley's fervent admirer and to the best of my ability fanned his fame. By 1940 Lady Rhondda had put at my disposal some space in her *Time & Tide* and whenever Arthur Waley published a new book, such as his *Monkey* and his *Three Ways of Thought in Ancient China*, I wrote long reviews in which I sought to present him as the scholar stylist of the moment. He had been a friend of Lytton Strachey's, not so close as Bernard Swithinbank, but a frequent visitor until Strachey's death in 1932, and so an associate of the Bloomsbury group. It is curious, however, that *The Tale of Genji* was not entirely to Strachey's taste. In a letter to Lady Ottoline Morrell in 1925, the date when its volume I was published, he wrote: 'Very beautiful in bits—country wine made by a lady of quality—cowslip brandy,'[1] a wicked understatement. The year 1940 was the time when Waley's lifelong friend, Beryl de Zoete, published her *Dance and Drama in Bali*, a book I also reviewed in *Time & Tide*, in a manner which even the author, not easy to please, agreed was complimentary. I was never able to become close friends with the two, for he was too remote, she too difficult, but the terms I reached sufficed to advance me in Far Eastern circles. I have a diary note, dated as early as 11th June 1939, describing how they both came to lunch at our house in Maidenhead. By then I had published *Siamese White* and three following books. In the review of Beryl de Zoete's book I had called Waley 'a fabulous scholar and poet' and her the author of 'a piece of creative writing of the first order'. In short, I was in good odour. Waley looked round my Chinese collection and seemed surprised at my having the lion-dog painting by Southern Duckweed. 'That's a very good picture,' he exclaimed almost disapprovingly as if I had no right to possess such a picture.

[1] See vol. 2, p. 515 of Michael Holroyd's *Biography of Lytton Strachey*.

After lunch I drove them to Professor Seligman's house at Toot Baldon, near Oxford. His collection of Chinese works of art was well known and very choice. He also wrote with authority on various aspects of Chinese culture. Encouraged by him, I was brought into contact with more people of that world, such as Gerald Reitlinger, C. P. Fitzgerald and Professor Yetts, who lectured at the Courtauld on early Chinese bronzes. They were free with good advice, without which I could hardly have dared to publish anything on so difficult and specialist a subject as China.

At this time I also became acquainted with S. I. Hsiung. He was not only Chinese in fact, instead of being English with a taste for things Chinese, but also a Chinese of very unusual gifts. I first met him in Dublin in 1935 immediately after my return from Mergui. His play, *Lady Precious Stream*, which had been running for some time with great acclaim in London, was on at the Dublin Gate Theatre. In a diary note written soon after the Dublin meeting I have: 'I induced him to dine with me. Mr Hsiung has had an extraordinary experience—a Chinese, he arrives friendless in London and writes or adapts a Chinese play, which looks like running indefinitely, an unheard of feat.' In an article in *Time & Tide* after Lady Rhondda had taken me up in 1939, I attempted to define further Mr. Hsiung's uniqueness. 'If you turn the case round and posit an Englishman writing plays in Chinese it helps. The supposed Englishman, very much of a supposition, takes one of our pre-Elizabethan Moralities, renders it into ideographs, has it played in Peking under his supervision, is hailed as an accomplished writer of Chinese by the Peking critics and sees his work translated into Japanese, Manchu, Siamese and Malay. That was Mr Hsiung's achievement—the other way round—and it is so out of this world that it is no exaggeration to call him today's most astonishing literary figure.'

When the above was written Hsiung had become friends with a wide circle of prominent people, including George Bernard Shaw and Lord Dunsany. He had produced two more plays and was writing a novel, *The Bridge of Heaven*, destined to be a best seller, for which John Masefield was to write an introductory poem. He had made enough money to bring his wife over from China, get a house near Oxford and begin to put his numerous children through the university. We became good friends and presently he suggested we should collaborate over a play on the famous Empress Dowager, Tzu Hsi, who died in 1908. I gladly accepted. Engaged as I was in reviewing for Lady Rhondda books on China and anxious to make China the subject of my next book, Hsiung's suggestion suited me very well. Moreover, I had a warm regard for him.

Before starting to collaborate with Hsiung I wrote my first book on China, a sketch of European relations with that country from A.D. 1600 to 1912, which I called *The Great Within*. So stated, the subject sounds extremely dull, but it turned out lively and amusing according to critics well placed to find fault with it. In November 1941 Mr. Hsiung himself wrote a leader in *Time & Tide*, declaring me to be accurate without being academic. Since Hsiung was a friend and *Time & Tide* a paper on which I had friends, his compliments could not be taken as wholly without an admixture of amiability. But a review a month later was to be quite impartial. I happened to run into Arthur Waley and Beryl de Zoete at some reception or other at the end of December 1941. She said: 'Have you seen Harold Acton's splendid review of your new book in the *Listener* today?' I said I had not and in a stupid way inquired who Harold Acton was. 'What!' she exclaimed, 'you mean to say you've never heard of Harold Acton!' She was much irritated by my ignorance. He was a close friend of Arthur Waley's and had the reputation of a clever writer. Moreover, he had resided for years in Peking, which was the central theme of my book, and was better qualified than anyone else in London to write an impartial and reliable review. That I had not come across him was partly due to his living chiefly in Florence. My not knowing even his name was damaging in the eyes of Beryl de Zoete, who interpreted it as revealing my subordinate position in the literary world. The fact was that I had been so busy writing that I had not gone about much. Harold Acton's review gave me a strong desire to know him, but I never got more than slightly acquainted with him because he was not often enough in London. He did me, however, an important service with his review. For a man of his standing—for he was very influential at the time—to write the way he did was extraordinary praise, considering that my knowledge of China was so limited. What information I had was gathered mostly from published English and French sources. The book was liked because it was written in a pleasing manner, as one might please people by the way one talked. Though published in the middle of the war, it sold well and launched me upon my new subject of China. What I had managed was essential for my future, for I was fifty-two years of age.

4

The play on the Empress Dowager

THE PREVIOUS CHAPTERS have shown how lucky I was after leaving Burma in 1934. Everything I turned to went well. But now the going was to be less easy.

In May 1941 Hsiung and I signed an agreement to cover our proposed collaboration. All profits were to be equally divided between us. Hsiung, however, made the condition that his name should not appear. The play was not to be advertised as by S. I. Hsiung and Maurice Collis, but as by me alone, copyright was to be in my name, and all contracts with publishers and producers to follow the same rule. It was no wish of mine that he stood out in this way. He desired it to be so, though what exactly were his reasons was never quite clear. I understood that as the play might reveal the Empress Dowager Tzu Hsi in a less flattering light than in books by previous English writers, it was possible that her admirers in China might prove embarrassing to Hsiung if his name appeared as joint author. But who could such objectors be? In 1941 the Japanese were in control of most of China. They were certainly no champions of Tzu Hsi and the Ch'ing dynasty which came to an end in 1912. Nor were the Chinese Nationalists, who had overthrown the dynasty and now under Chiang Kai Shek were holding out in a north-west corner of the country. It is true that the Japanese had made Tzu Hsi's grand-nephew, Henry Pu-Yi, Emperor of Manchukuo. But was it conceivable that he would take umbrage? It was not conceivable. But for some reason or other caution made Hsiung keep his name out twenty-seven years ago. I assume that he cannot be apprehensive now, and that

I may proceed to explain how he and I got on as collaborators.

Hsiung's chief task was to supply the original Chinese sources on which to construct the Empress Dowager's career. These sources had never been translated into English. Without some Chinese helper I would have had nothing to go on except books like Backhouse and Bland's *China under the Empress Dowager*, published some thirty years before, when sources now available were not to hand. To produce in English excerpts from these sources was Hsiung's first concern. He was an experienced dramatist. His *Lady Precious Stream* had been performed in the West End hundreds of times. He had written other plays and in China had had practical experience with play production. His English was good, quite extraordinarily good for a Chinese. One wonders, then, why he asked me to collaborate with him. Was I to be merely a ghost, a name behind which he could hide? Or did he admire my style and believe I would do better than he could? If the latter was his reason for asking my help, it is very flattering. My *Great Within* had given me, I suppose, some reputation in the China field. But his reputation as a dramatist in that field was far greater. I never added all this up, but got to work cheerfully on the collaboration, reading his translations of the sources, drafting scene after scene, receiving his emendations, discussing with him problems as they arose, and clothing the agreed facts in my own style, for I was incapable of writing in any other. My style was unlike the manner he invented for *Lady Precious Stream*, so unlike that when his inclination was to bring in a bit in the Precious Stream vein of fancy, I had to resist. But there was no difficulty with Hsiung. His emendations were excellent and I embodied them. That is how the play was evolved.

It immediately attracted the attention of the actor, John Gielgud, who at that time was at the height of his reputation. We were very delighted. I had a pleasant chat with him and reported his interest to Faber & Faber, who were on the point of publishing the play in book form under the title of *The Motherly and Auspicious*, a translation of the name Tzu Hsi. I discovered, however, that I was going too fast in assuming that what Gielgud had said to me meant acceptance of the play. On 15th June 1943 he wrote: 'I was a little surprised last week to receive a letter from Messrs Faber & Faber suggesting that I should take an option on *The Motherly and Auspicious*. I am sorry if I have ever given the impression that I would like to acquire the play.' And he went on to explain that he merely directed plays which the firm of H. N. Tennent bought for production. Tennent's manager was Hugh Beaumont, whose reaction to the play had first to be ascertained. 'Of course,' added Gielgud, 'I very much hope that he will like the play sufficiently to acquire it, and ask me to direct it for him. . . . The more I see of the play, the more I feel that it could be made into a very distinguished and interesting production.'

To an inexperienced person like myself this looked good enough. Surely if Gielgud wanted to do the play he could get Beaumont to acquire it. Hsiung with his greater experience of the theatrical background was not so naïvely sanguine. From his different world Bernard Swithinbank wondered too. In a letter from him (17/5/43) was the amusing latinish sentence: 'I hope the play will fix the capricious affections of the histrions.'

When Mr. Beaumont came to examine the play he was startled by the number of scenes and characters: thirteen scenes, and twenty-nine characters, amounted to a very tall order. Nevertheless, in July an option of £100 was taken, a small sum but sufficient to hold the play at the producers' disposal for a few months while they made up their minds. In the course of the autumn they came to the conclusion that it would be too difficult to stage. Gielgud also was said to have lost some of his original enthusiasm. The deal was off.

We were very disappointed. But some other management might take it up. It would be tedious to recount the negotiations which followed, to name the several actresses, some very well known, who were keen to get the leading part, and to detail the number of options which were paid and led nowhere. Suffice it to say that the play, in spite of efforts lasting over seventeen years, was never produced in the West End, though it had several provincial productions.

It was published, however, in book form by Faber & Faber in November 1943. As a rule it is difficult to sell a play which has not been produced. Fabers took the risk and were successful. It sold over two thousand copies in the first two months. The press was cordial. Veronica Wedgwood, then a rising historian of note, with three admirable books published and another, *William the Silent*, on the point of coming out, reviewed the play in *Time & Tide*, where she was Lady Rhondda's colleague. She found it astonishing, she said. As an historian she was struck by how much more tension a narrative, founded on fact, but fictionalized in the form of a drama, was capable of conveying than an historian writing straight could convey. That was a great deal for a professional historian to admit. Tsui Chi, a Chinese scholar resident in England whose book *A Short History of Chinese Civilisation* had just appeared and was being widely read, published a letter in *Time & Tide* in which he emphasized that the sources used by Hsiung were reliable and had long been accepted by scholars in China. Lionel Giles also gave his support. He was examiner in Chinese to the University of Cambridge and had been a colleague of Arthur Waley's in the British Museum. He attached sufficient importance to the play, as throwing new light on Tzu Hsi, to ask me to lecture to the China Society, of which he was honorary secretary.

Meanwhile a storm blew up. J. O. P. Bland, the joint author with E. Backhouse (not alive in 1943) of *China under the Empress Dowager*, published in 1914, became indignant. His book was well written and had quite a vogue in its day. But it was now out of date because of the new sources above mentioned, which revealed Tzu Hsi as a much more formidable and sinister character than he depicted. In the later editions of his book, he had made no reference to any new sources. He seems not to have heard of any or to have dismissed them as scurrilous and not worth reading. The fact was that he did not know Chinese and was not in touch with what was current in Peking. His book had kept the field and he enjoyed for years the reputation of a distinguished man of letters. It so happened that no sinologue addressed himself seriously to the task of writing a biography of Tzu Hsi between 1914, the date of his book, and 1943 when my play was published. In my preface to it I was obliged to refer to his book as having

Maurice Collis, 1939, aged fifty

marked limitations. It gave a picture of Tzu Hsi which was irreconcilable with the Chinese memoirs I listed. To defend his reputation as a brilliant writer on Chinese court life he rushed in rashly and declared in the press that my account of the Empress Dowager was wholly fictional. 'Hollywood history' he called it. It was known that I had a collaborator acquainted with Chinese. Who was he? demanded Mr. Bland. Let him reveal himself and describe fully the nature of the sources he had supplied. If there were such sources—hard to believe since he, Bland, had never heard of them—they no doubt had been doctored to tickle the popular taste of England and America. The suggestion was that I had vilified for mercenary reasons one of the greatest and most admired women in Chinese history. Mr. Bland was now elderly and irascible. He was not going to see his masterpiece, *China under the Empress Dowager*, belittled by an ex-Indian Civilian, a class of man notoriously ignorant of Far Eastern history, indeed of everything outside the narrow field of Indian administration.

This onslaught appeared to me so patently idiotic that my inclination was to ignore it. But Mr. Bland now started writing me personal letters of an abusive kind. When at first I did not reply, his letters became threatening. He seemed to have lost his head. He was not dangerous, for he had no case, but he had become a sad bore. Accordingly I addressed a letter to *The Times Literary Supplement* in which he had reviewed *The Motherly and Auspicious* and pointed out the fundamental weakness of his criticisms in that he had not read, or had neglected to get read for him, the new sources I had adduced, all of which were by persons of consequence and integrity, some even writers of prescribed texts for university students in China. I was also glad to accept Lionel Giles's kind invitation to address the China Society. The lecture, subsequently published by the Society, was chaired by Professor Yetts of the Courtauld Institute and among the audience were the Chinese Ambassador and Madame Wellington Koo. He had been foreign minister in the Nationalist Government and now represented the Republic at the Court of St. James. Madame Wellington Koo had read *The Great Within* and liked to declare that to write it I must have lived for years in Peking or I could not otherwise have described the city so accurately. Her dislike of Mr. Bland was ferocious; at the close of my lecture she remarked to me with satisfaction that it would be the end of him. Anyhow it shut him up. He wrote no more to the press or to me. His death followed a year later.

5

Chips and Wavell

WHILE THIS ATTEMPT to establish myself as a playwright was in progress, I had written another book, which was published at the beginning of 1943, thus preceding the publication of *The Motherly and Auspicious* by nine months. The book was *The Land of the Great Image*, its main theme the adventures of a Portuguese monk in Arakan, a part of Burma which was then an independent Buddhist kingdom on the eastern frontiers of Bengal. Though a return to the subject of Burma, it was totally different in matter from my former books on that country. Geoffrey Faber gave a larger advance than before— £300—which was immediately recouped, as it sold over three thousand five hundred copies in four months. An English film company paid £500 for rights and it was taken by an American publisher. The book had been long maturing. Its foundations were laid in 1924 when as Deputy Commissioner in Arakan I had gone over the ground, studied the Arakanese chronicles with the help of my learned friend, U San Shwe Bu, read the monk's memoirs, and published a series of essays in the *Burma Research Journal*, an early excursion into Burmese history which earned me the rebuke in official quarters referred to in earlier pages. Now nearly twenty years later I returned to the theme, confident that I was at last experienced enough to write a full narration of what were certainly very singular events. They were so singular, however, and connected with a part of the world so little known and with persons never heard of before, whose beliefs, steeped in magic, were exceedingly alien, that it was a question whether the English public would care for such a book. I liked the haunted background and the then King of Arakan's phantasmal character. In *The Dark Door* I had drawn a fictional picture of such a Burmese sub-world; now in *The Land of the Great Image* I was dealing with it as history. The book, however, attracted the general reader and did not outrage professional orientalists. For myself it exactly suited my relish for men and events which were superreal. The great soup of human hearts, boiled to make an elixir able to deflect the astrological dilemma facing the king, was the sort of accessory I felt at home with.

The book brought me into touch with people prominent in London society whom I had not met before and whose goodwill was to prove valuable to me as a writer. Two quotations from Henry Channon's[1] diaries will serve to introduce this turn in my fortunes. The first is dated 30th May 1943, about six months after the publication of *The Land of the Great Image*. Chips Channon knew everyone in society from the Royal Family downwards and his wealth permitted him to give very good parties in his town house, 5 Belgrave Square, and at Kelvedon in Essex. His London dining-room was a splendid apartment, modelled on a rococo masterpiece in the Amalienburg, a palace of the Ludwigs of Bavaria, whose family he knew well and of whom he wrote a history, *The Ludwigs of Bavaria*, published in 1933. Before May 1943, the date of the first diary entry in question, I had not met him. It relates of an occasion when he went to St. Pancras railway station to see off Field Marshal Lord Wavell, then Commander-in-Chief in India, shortly to become Viceroy of India. 'I piloted Wavell to the train where we were received by General Paget, C in C Home Forces, and taken aboard, and given drinks in the luxurious saloon. They begged me to come along, but I had no luggage. I put Maurice Collis's book, *The Land of the Great Image*, in the Field Marshal's wagon-lit and then finally left, driving home in his grand car.'

The second quotation is dated several weeks later (20th July 1943): 'The Field Marshal and Lady Wavell, he wearing my black striped suit, and Lady Wavell in a hat I think she had made herself, lunched at Buckingham Palace, while I lunched with Sibyl Cole-

[1] *Chips. The Diaries of Sir Henry Channon.* Edited by R. James, 1967.

fax and Diana Cooper at the Ivy.[1] Sibyl had collected Maurice
Collis for me whom I so wanted to meet. He is my new literary
hero, and author of those absorbing books, *The Great Within*,
Siamese White and others. In appearance he is a typical retired
civil servant, which for many years he was. Luckily he got into
some scrape and resigned, so literature is the richer.'

Chips was a man with aspirations to ministerial office and had
been an M.P. for years. But his dominant interest lay in acquaintance with the leading people of the day, entertaining them at his
table, and getting them to talk of what was going on behind the
scenes. He liked to get guests who were in the news at the
moment. His house in that way became a centre for amusing
gossip. The guests enjoyed themselves for it was never boring. His
flair for picking the right people made him the best host in
London. His reason for inviting me to lunch at the Ivy was
because my books had made me favourably spoken of. Besides
that, he himself was genuinely delighted with them. It was my
first assurance, outside the newspapers and the congratulations of
friends, that I had got somewhere.

His idea of some scrape or other was no doubt acquired in
casual talk—Maurice Collis had resigned because the authorities
in Burma had complained of this and that and were displeased
with him. Actually, as I have mentioned farther back, there was no
scrape beyond a difference of opinion on the trend of events. I had
left because I saw no future. The scrape idea had grown, besides, a
little old-fashioned, as by 1943 my views had become ordinary
commonplaces. Chips uses the word 'luckily' in his diary entry,
pretending my retirement was lucky for literature. The real luck
was that I myself was lucky. Chips liked me and, in spite of my
appalling resemblance to a retired civil servant, decided to invite
me to his house.

Within a month or so of the Ivy lunch, Lord Wavell was
appointed Viceroy of India, then threatened by Japanese invasion,

[1] Sibyl Colefax, whose lunches and dinners for prominent people were a
feature of the London social round. Lady Diana Cooper, daughter of the Duke
of Rutland, wife of Duff Cooper, Cabinet Minister and later Ambassador in
Paris.

for their forces stood on the borders of Manipur and Chittagong. On the eve of his departure, Chips arranged a luncheon for him, to which I was invited. Lady Diana Cooper was there. I was presented to the Wavells. Lady Wavell had heard talk of my play, *The Motherly and Auspicious*, for Gielgud still talked of producing it. 'Come out and stay with us,' said she. 'We'll have your play put on at Simla.' It was one of those tantalizingly impossible invitations.

On taking over charge at Delhi, Wavell went to visit the British front against the Japanese in northern Arakan. He wrote to Chips, so Chips told me: 'I'm off to the Collis country,' showing he had read and remembered *The Land of the Great Image*, which Chips had slipped into his wagon-lit in June. What a move up for me who in 1925 had been rebuked for writing about Arakan!

I never met Wavell and his wife again, Wavell so remote, so silent, so mysterious apparently, but underneath so rich a personality. His book *Other Men's Flowers* was published the very day of Chips's luncheon. I rushed round afterwards to Hatchards and bought it, a delightful collection of rousing verses, all of which he was reputed to have by heart.

Chips continued to invite me to luncheons and I grew to take for granted his hospitality, which I was far too poor to return except by making myself as obliging as possible to him and his guests, who included on one occasion the Duchess of Kent and her children. 'What lovely manners they have!' I said to her. She smiled with a politeness it was impossible to better, showing simultaneously pleasure at the compliment and a hint of doubt whether they fully deserved it.

I got to like Chips, as was only natural since he was so kind. But quite unexpectedly a year or two later I heard that he felt that I did not reciprocate his liking. He had invited me again and again, but I had never asked him back. Well, it never had occurred to me that he expected this. I had no means of entertaining him in the style to which he was accustomed. I hastened round to call. I found him, however, a little stiff. I could not soothe him altogether. Perhaps it was just his state of health, which was not as good as it had been. In 1943 he was forty-six to my fifty-four. In succeeding years he suffered several heart attacks but lasted till his sixty-first year in 1958. On his headstone at Kelvedon was inscribed the line from Du Bellay: 'Heureux qui comme Ulysse a fait un beau voyage', a line I had quoted in my *Siamese White* as summing up Samuel White's reflections in 1687 as he sailed home to England where shortly afterwards he died, the line serving, as it were, as an epitaph for him.

A couple of years ago I was brought up by Sir Gilbert Laithwaite to speak to the Duchess of Kent (by then the Princess Marina) in the Colonial Institute where she had just opened an exhibition. I reminded her we had once met at Chips's luncheon table over twenty years before. She recalled the occasion, or induced me to believe so. She had known Chips well; she and the Duke lived next door in Belgrave Square. There was a gentle tone of amused indulgence in her voice as she said: 'Ah, poor Chips,' for her recollection of him, despite his social prominence, was of a man who was a little disappointed.

6

I become an art critic

I ADDED TO MY labours in May 1941 by becoming art critic for
Lady Rhondda's *Time & Tide*. She had been publishing my book
reviews since 1939. Now twice a month I let her have my opinion
of the London exhibitions. The pay was trifling, but I enjoyed the
job. My qualifications were slender. Lady Rhondda was on the
look-out for an art critic of some sort, admired my books, thought
my literary reviews lively, and that I would do. I had been
interested in pictures for years, possessed a collection of my own,
and during my leaves from Burma had stayed in Paris, the world's
art centre, and took in all I could. But I had little real claim to be a
professional critic. My only asset was an eye, the collector's eye,
which detects quality, an instinctive gift.

So I started off, inexperienced but eager, into the art world, not
for money or reputation, but for the love of the thing. In a diary
entry a few months later I have: 'I did not anticipate that my notes
would attract any attention. I had no axe to grind, no party to
support, no theory to push, and no novelties for a sensational
entry on the scene. My object was to write soberly and to be
guided more by sensibility than doctrine.' I found it a great
relaxation.

At this date Roger Fry had just died and the most prominent
art critics were Clive Bell, another of Lytton Strachey's friends,
Herbert Read, poet, theorist and champion of the French
modernists, Sir Kenneth Clark, Director of the National Gallery,
and R. H. Wilenski, art historian. The best-known working critic
was Eric Newton of the *Sunday Times*. These were all men of long

experience in the arts and may have hardly noticed my intrusion, unless my books gave them pause. I had at least the advantage of having read much of what they had published. Moreover, since 1935 I had frequented the London galleries regularly. But as I have said, I had little more than an eye, and that not fully trained.

What I wrote was amateurish and overbuoyant in a youthful manner, but I succeeded in picking out here and there artists later to be celebrated. In one of my first reviews I wrote of Stanley Spencer. I had first seen a painting of his when just back from Burma I went to the 1935 Academy. Wandering round the exhibition I came on his picture 'Workmen in the House'. My diary has: 'Two lively girls, art students evidently, arrived. "Oh, there's Stanley!" says one. "He's all jumbled up as usual but he gets there," says the other. "Abominable hanging," says the first, pointing to Spencer's position between two academic landscapes. "Done on purpose, I shouldn't wonder." "Nor should I," agrees the second, "but I must say I've never seen a plumber in foot-ball boots before." I looked. The workman with the saw *had* football boots. After this the rest of the exhibition was less interesting.'[1]

In 1935 Stanley Spencer was already well known. His quarrel with the Academy and resignation a few days before I saw his 'Workmen in the House' had made him the most talked of artist in London. Between 1935 and my first mention of him in *Time & Tide* in April 1941 he painted all his famous erotic pictures. The originality and importance of these were not understood. There is no trace in my notes on him to show that I grasped his significance. 'At Tooths', I wrote, 'are two Stanley Spencers, *Priory Farm* and *Purple Clematis*, of moderate size and moderate price, but far more than moderately good. In their quality, colour, boldness and sanity they are superb examples of his latest work.' This was a misapprehension. They were pot-boilers, exhibited by Tooth because he knew he could sell them and because he did not like and could not sell the real Stanley Spencer as revealed in his recent subliminal creations. Beside these great visionary canvases 'Priory Farm' and 'Purple Clematis' were commonplace, their colour and

[1] Quoted from diary dated 7 May 1935.

quality unremarkable, boldness not their characteristic and their sanity quite ordinary. It was nonsense to put them forward as superb examples of his latest work. But such at the moment was the view that generally prevailed. Though I got to know him personally in the fifties, it was not until after his death in 1959 when I had the chance, as will be related, to read his private papers, that I understood the meaning of his principal paintings.

In this early exploration of the London art world I made the acquaintance of several painters already eminent or destined to become so. One of these was Topolski. My first note on him in *Time & Tide* (19/7/41) has: 'A most individual artist. His amusing or satiric drawings have no resemblance to the work of any artist, alive or dead. The inner life of his faces, the whirligig of his draperies and his macabre legs belong to a fantastic world of their own. *Charles II and his spaniel* has the appearance these two would take on if one day you saw them disappearing round a corner at Hampton Court.' I was frequently in his studio after that and gradually made a collection of his drawings and oils.

The work of L. S. Lowry attracted me from the first. Though he had been painting for years he came on to the London scene only in 1939 after Mr. Reid of the Reid Lefevre Gallery had come across a number of his pictures at Bourlets, the London framers. The first of his paintings I saw was at a mixed exhibition in August 1942 and my comment was: 'Mr Lowry has his own vision. The critics I do not think have pushed him enough. He is a very English painter.' His prices were low; for £20 one could buy a picture. In 1943 he had his second exhibition in his patron, Mr. Reid's, gallery. I had begun to feel strongly about him. I wrote: 'Mr Lowry is essentially an English artist, one of our very few. Yet he has been made less fuss of than men with half his talent.' While other artists had been warmly commended for pictures in one of the current French styles, he had been working quietly in urban Lancashire and 'transforming a reality of back streets, ragamuffins, courtyards, football, towpaths and tenements into feeling and beauty. In short, what you have got is a little English master.' I was the first critic to make this claim in a London newspaper. It had some effect, but not much. Sir Kenneth Clark, who at this time was using empty rooms in the National Gallery to exhibit paintings by war artists, did not include Lowry. It was true that Lowry, by now a man of sixty, had not been sent overseas to paint the war effort, but nothing could have been more suitable than one of his industrial landscapes in the midlands to represent the working classes whose dogged exertions made our victory possible. Lowry was only gradually taken up by the critics and the public. His work could still be bought very cheap; paintings now costing anything from £3,000 to £8,000, being priced below £100.

It might seem that writing art reviews was an innocuous occupation. You couldn't always please artists and dealers, but if you were clearly trying to be fair and agreeable, you were excused an occasional disparaging remark. I did not escape, however, a row with the artist and writer Wyndham Lewis. This happened after his return to England from America, where he had spent the war years. He was best known as a ferocious satirist. In his *The Apes of God* (1931), for instance, he had shown himself the arch-enemy of the Bloomsbury group, lampooning with formidable power the three Sitwells, and also Lytton Strachey in the character of Matthew Plunkett, a degraded and idiotic *poseur*. He was feared and hated by many people. I never met him to speak to, but on one occasion the way he prowled round the Leicester Galleries attracted my attention. Not sure at first that it was he, I asked one of the directors who was nervously watching from the side. He told me, and I asked: 'Has he mellowed at all?' 'Not in the least,' said the director, 'and I advise you to give him a wide berth. You can't talk to him. He jumps down your throat.' Well, it was this warrior, stained with the blood of countless fights, that I fell foul of. In 1946 he exhibited a couple of paintings in pastel and chalk in the Lefevre Gallery. He was then aged sixty and his reputation as a painter was comparable to what he enjoyed as a writer. But the paintings in this case were trifles and I suggested in *Time & Tide* that he might have let us see something more representative of his art. But unwilling to show work of importance he might have done in America, he exhibited again next year in the same gallery what I called 'a slender display of five drawings'. In January of the next year he had one painting at the Leicester Galleries. My note was: 'Wyndham Lewis finds himself in the awkward situation of an old revolutionary, whose blasts no longer startle.' It was known that his eyesight was failing. His more recent books had not the fierce bite of his best period, the thirties.

This third reflection on the pictures he had shown since returning to England roused him to fury. He wrote to the editor of *Time & Tide* that it was evidently impossible for him to exhibit a painting or a drawing without my delivering myself of an offensive inanity. He called me a 'Sahib turned picture-pundit' who was ludicrously ignorant of what he was writing about and quite without the modesty he should show considering that he had only been invented by Lady Rhondda. And he ended, almost pathetically, by complaining of my pertinacious ill-will towards him, as if it could matter what an ex-Indian Civilian said.

My reply was published in *Time & Tide* on 7th February 1948. 'I must thank Mr Wyndham Lewis for abusing me. For a man who has spent twenty years in a mangrove swamp it is a great honour to be noticed at all by so grand a gentleman. Had anyone told me in the old swamp times that the day would come when Mr Wyndham Lewis would condescend to reach down and have a hit at me, I should have been happier than I was.' And I went on to say that my Burma loneliness had been enlivened by his books, which were regularly posted to me from London. He was, in fact, one of my favourite authors. What would delight me would be to see a retrospective exhibition of all his paintings.

This was the end of the altercation. Whether he was pulled up by my banter or put in better humour by my respect for his writings, I cannot say. But thereafter there was silence. The affair much amused the *Time & Tide* people, I was told. They took it as a lively high-level exchange. Lady Rhondda used on occasion to give literary parties. When the drinks had gone round—she used to lace her champagne with brandy—guests enjoyed a good laugh at Wyndham Lewis's expense. His attainments as a writer and an artist were not denied, but there was something ridiculous about his irascibility.

During the war I continued with assiduity to do my art reviews for *Time & Tide*. In January 1945 the *Observer* asked me to write on art for them also for a while. Lady Rhondda had no objection provided I continued as before to write art reviews for her. In a generous and warm-hearted way she remarked that she took it as a compliment the *Observer* had to draw on her staff. So I shouldered the double work and sought to make my reviews independent of each other. The remuneration was very bad, but it gave me a leg up in public estimation.

Just before this I came upon Mervyn Peake. He was thirty-three years of age, had been invalided out of the army and was writing his *Titus Groan*, the first of the trilogy which made him famous. As a poet he had already a name. I would sometimes stroll with him up the King's Road, and I remember how once he pulled out of his pocket a sheaf of pencilled poems and read me one, the now much admired lament which begins:

> *The paper is breathless*
> *Under the hand*
> *And the pencil is poised*
> *Like a warlock's wand.*

We were turning into Sloane Square and a sudden gust plucked the poem from his hand and sent it fluttering across the street. As we tried to recover it he was prompted to say: 'The poet cries his ghostly manifesto upon the world and who cares when the wind lets it drop in the dirt?' In July 1944 he had his first comprehensive exhibition of drawings and paintings. It was held in Peter Jones's shop in Sloane Square. Hitherto the art critics had taken small notice when an occasional drawing of his was hung in the West End, though in the thirties, when he was twenty-five, the *London Mercury* had published one or two of his line drawings. It was his line drawings that particularly attracted me at Peter Jones. I wrote with an enthusiasm more than justified later on: 'I know of no one alive who could achieve such line drawings,' and I referred in particular to one where a huge muscular man holds up on a tray, as if with great effort, a tiny flower. 'Mr Peake has laid his cards on the table. I point to that one. It is an ace of trumps. He can make a fortune by it.'

Mervyn Peake was not the sort of man to make a fortune, but

with his drawings, his poems and his truly astounding creations, *Titus Groan* and *Gormenghast*, he made a name which is still growing. It was some time, however, before he won the suffrages of the critics and when he died in 1968, aged fifty-seven, he was very poor, though rich in achievements as artist and writer.

I continued altogether for ten years to contribute regularly to *Time & Tide* reviews of current exhibitions and touched on the work of no less than 490 artists by name. This greatly increased my knowledge of the subject and of the world, for I met and profited by the friendship of many remarkable men and women, such as Henry Moore, Dora Gordine, Cecil Collins, John Piper and Julian Trevelyan. Otherwise my books, concerned up till 1950 with oriental matters, might have had a restricting effect on my mind and relegated me to the society of orientalists in museums, academies, clubs and the like. As it was, my circle of friends and acquaintances was wide and I was saved from becoming an oriental specialist, which would certainly have been to my detriment as a writer.

I was very lucky during the war. I noted on VE Day (Victory in Europe): 'My household and I during these last five years which have wrecked Europe and caused hideous disasters, despairs, separations and deaths, have lived here in Maidenhead quite untouched. Our food has been sufficient, our health good, our life unchanged, our spirits normal. The bombs which have fallen near us were far off enough to be harmless. I record this good fortune with profound humility.'

One of the great protagonists of the war passed within a few yards of our door on 19th October 1945. 'At 11 a.m. I went to see Field Marshal Montgomery enter to receive the freedom of Maidenhead. In battle dress, a black beret on his head, he alighted from his car and shook hands with the Mayor, Mr Oldershaw. After standing for a moment under the Union Jack, while the guard of honour of the Berkshires saluted him, he walked slowly among the ranks. I was in the crowd not more than a few feet from him and was able to study his face. It was more worn than I expected, much lined round the eyes. These were very piercing. As he paused in his inspection to speak with the soldiers, he looked up at them, his eyes very brilliant, yet his expression sweet and sad, a strange sadness. The men were gravely embarrassed, as if spoken to by a god, and seemed in a sort of trance of fearful happiness. The spectators were very quiet, and gazed on him with an intense concentration, for he was more thrilling to watch than any actor upon a stage. Why was he sad, if sad he were? Had the adulation lavished on him by the nation led him to perceive the vanity of vanities? Who can say? The rite of the inspection over, he drove on up the street, standing in his car and saluting the people. In their eyes he was a victorious General in a moment of triumph; to me he looked like an Irish gentleman.'

The emotion with which this glimpse of Montgomery was written reveals the strain we had all been under, our relief and thankfulness.

In the summer of 1946 I paid a fortnight's visit to Paris to find out, if I could, the art situation there. Were new movements afoot? In short, what was the latest news? One had to bring oneself up to date. Had any new painters of merit made their appearance? I had good introductions. Peter Gimpel, a director of Gimpel Fils, a recently established West End art gallery, was in Paris at the moment and promised to help me to meet the right people. The British Council's representative, Mr. McEwen, was ready to do the same. Apparently I was the first of the London art reviewers to see the advantage of an exploration of post-war Paris. Peter Gimpel had a car and at once took me to call on his friends. I accompanied him to the Gallery Mouradian, rue de Seine, where he hoped to secure some paintings by Soutine, who had recently died before attracting much notice. Peter Gimpel, however, was convinced that he was a master. I was shown two paintings which 'in cleanness of paint and fluidity of brush made a great impression on me', as I put it in my diary. His prices at the Gallery Mouradian were only a fraction of what they became a few years later. I saw Peter Gimpel buying one of his best paintings for £400.

It soon became clear that the question to which I sought an answer—who were the new painters likely to make big names—was one which no one could answer. The British Council and

Gimpel's friends, pointing out that there were 200 dealers' galleries in Paris at least, declared it was impossible to tell offhand what latent genius might lurk there. However, to oblige me, I was taken at once to the studios of two supposedly promising painters, Pignon and Fougeron. But I was unable to detect sufficient original talent in either to allow me to conclude that they represented what I had come over to find.

One time I broke away from my conductors and slipped into the Louvre to refresh my eyes with the masterpieces I had not seen for five years. 'The Gioconda, the Venus of Milo and the Winged Victory were in their places and worked their charm as if nothing had happened and there had never been a Hitler,' I noted. 'To see them and the great pictures by Correggio, Titian, Rubens and Velazquez was like coming home after a long journey. The tears flowed freely.' I also felt a longing to see again the Cham sculptures at the Guimet, of all South East Asian art the most delightful in my view. I found their divinities roguishly smiling. Hitler was dead; both for gods and men it was a time to smile.

But I could not indulge myself in this fashion for long and was soon accompanying Mr. McEwen to the Carré gallery. Here to explain one of the exhibits a member of the staff recited a piece of art patter I found very fetching. The painter, he said, was 'inspired by Cubist intellectual ideas to a non-intellectuality, as if he had been thrown into a vision by a mathematical equation'. It was like a quotation from a Mahayanist sutra.

The next day, however, I saw the work of an artist who was destined to become a name, though I was not clever enough to perceive this. I was chatting to M. Carlhian, the celebrated interior decorator, the kindest to me of all Peter Gimpel's friends, in his magnificent premises in the Place Vendôme. He suggested I should look in at the Drouin gallery on the other side of the square, where I would see the very latest thing. When I got there I was shown by the director, 'an elegant man of about forty, very jumpy, with a curious snarling smile and the manners of a conjuror, pictures consisting of masses of glue and gravel, plastered over with a coloured substance on which were inscribed faces and forms'. They were by Dubuffet; he had not yet been properly

Louise Collis in 1950

launched on his voyage to the international reputation he now enjoys. The man with the smile assured me that Dubuffet would surely rise, but I did not believe him. So it was that when shown the new sort of painter I had come over to look for, I was unable to sense that, even though I could see nothing in his glue and gravel, a taste for it existed, to which he was responding, and which would suffice to make him the rage. Since then we have seen much stranger divagations from the norm.

With the end of the war a demand for French translations of my books had begun and the visit afforded me opportunity of calling on publishers who had shown interest, particularly on M. Calmann-Lévy. He paid me the compliment of inviting me to a family lunch at one of those restaurants which on the outside look like an ordinary brasserie, but have a noted cuisine, are frequented by French epicures and are unknown to English tourists. I suppose that the meal I was given was the best I had eaten for years, for apart from the cooking, food in Paris, despite all the sufferings of the German occupation, was much better than in London. M. Calmann-Lévy brought out a French translation of *The Great Within* shortly afterwards.

When Lady Diana Cooper, whom I had not seen since the lunch with Chips in 1943, heard I was in Paris, she invited me to dinner at the embassy; Duff Cooper had been ambassador for about a year. I was happy to go, for like everyone who met her I found her delightful. It was a small party, about six, including Peter Quennell. In my diary note I have: 'Lady Diana entered dressed in an evening gown, and looking the same as always, with the characteristic startled expression, which Cecil Beaton had caught so well in a drawing of her which was on the wall. As the weather was very hot, the dinner table was in a veranda room opening direct on a floodlit garden. The setting was luxurious, the dinner, to my starved eyes, a marvel. Lady Diana told me some of her adventures during the war, of her visit to Rangoon[1] in 1941 and of her escape from Singapore with Duff Cooper before it fell to the Japanese. Since I had seen her last, she had been to India to stay with Wavell and had actually visited the front in Arakan,

---

[1] See my *Last and First in Burma*, p. 41.

which had given my *The Land of the Great Image* an added interest for her. This led her to declare to the dinner party that I was her favourite author, a compliment which possibly she seriously meant, as she would not otherwise have said it before Peter Quennell. Duff Cooper, detained at a session of the Big Four, came in after we had started dinner. He was very pleasant to me. Some time before I had heard that at a dinner in Singapore in 1941, where he had been sent by Churchill to inquire into the city's preparedness against possible attack, he had advised Tony Keswick,[1] who was dining with him, to get me to write a book on the early days of the firm of Jardine and Matheson. This led to my being shown the firm's records and enabled me to write *Foreign Mud* which was published in 1946. On my asking Duff Cooper whether he had told Tony Keswick to do this, so that I might thank him, he said he had. It was an amusing and friendly occasion, for I felt that these interesting people had a regard for me. The party broke up at midnight and they drove me back to my hotel.

During the European war one was free, of course, to visit Ireland, my native land. My father and mother were still alive, living in the house, Kilmore, standing on the hill-side overlooking Killiney bay, with a view of the Wicklow mountains on the southern horizon. I made the journey at least twice a year and became acquainted with Victor Waddington, who at that time had an excellent art gallery in Anne Street, Dublin, where the best of Irish painting was exhibited. He was the man who first realized that Jack Yeats, the brother of W. B. Yeats, the poet, was a great artist and he set himself to advance his name by all means in his power. I entirely agreed with his estimate and deplored that Jack Yeats was not more thought of in London, where a painting of his could be bought for £20 or so, the same as Lowry's in the early forties. His brother, the poet, had already an international reputation. Jack Yeats was a more lonely figure. During my visits to Dublin I used to call on him about six when he had returned from his habitual solitary walk. His house was at the south corner of

[1] W. J. Keswick, chairman of Matheson & Co., and a Director of the Bank of England.

FitzWilliam Square. The studio was on the first floor. Though quite commodious, it seemed small because it was cut up by partitions, behind which he kept his painting and his whisky. McCreevy, Director of the Irish National Gallery, was often there at such an hour, when he was given the task of pouring out the whisky. Jack Yeats's air was reserved and dignified. I have never seen any painter in London treated with the deference accorded him, not even the President of the Royal Academy in his own circle. When the whisky had been round once or twice, he used to withdraw behind a partition and bring out in succession canvas after canvas, which he placed in a frame, behind glass, and displayed on an easel. The frames were large and heavy, but he refused assistance, though an old man in his seventies. As I admired his painting and found him personally charming and interesting these occasions were very enjoyable.

Victor Waddington in due course moved to London and was able to push Jack Yeats so successfully that before his death he was getting prices which, though much below what his paintings cost now, were many times higher than he used to get in Dublin.

In 1938 W. B. Yeats, the poet, had died at Menton on the French Riviera. The Irish Government, feeling that as he was the greatest poet in Irish history his grave ought to be in Ireland, obtained leave to disinter his body and bring it to Ireland. Among his poems was the famous one beginning:

> *Under bare Ben Bulben's head*
> *In Drumcliffe churchyard Yeats is laid . . .*

which was interpreted as his wish to be buried at Drumcliffe, a little graveyard near Sligo. In 1948 the government sent a naval corvette to Menton to fetch his body. Anxious to attend the funeral at Drumcliffe, I went over to Dublin on 15th September 1948. My brother, Bob Collis, offered to drive me across to Sligo on the 17th, the day the body was due to arrive. Louis MacNeice had also come over and my brother offered him a seat in the car. MacNeice had many friends in Dublin and was lavishly entertained by them on the evening of the 16th. We were supposed to leave Dublin at 7.30 a.m. on the 17th, but it was 8.30 before he put in an appearance at 26 FitzWilliam Square, my brother's house. He had a dreadful hangover. His large eyes were not quite open. We stuffed him into the back of the car along with Maurice Craig, another poet, for all the poets of Ireland, great and small, were setting out for Yeats's funeral that day. We drove fast to Longford. The Earl had gone on and we stopped for coffee, bread and butter and marmalade at the Longford Arms. There we were joined by Austin Clarke, the poet. By 12.45 we were entering Sligo town, and overtook the funeral cortège. The body of Yeats had been landed at Galway that morning and transferred to a waiting motor hearse, which when we came on it outside Sligo was escorted by a band of Irish pipers.

Turning off down a side street we reached the Town Hall ahead of the funeral procession and took our stand on the Town Hall's steps. A large crowd filled the square. A guard of honour from an Irish regiment, in khaki and tin helmets, under an officer who gave his orders in Gaelic, cleared a space, where the hearse came to a stop. Behind the hearse we now saw cars in which were Yeats's wife and daughter, Ann, and the painter, his brother, Jack Yeats.

A halt was now made for lunch, while the guard stood to attention round the coffin with arms reversed. By this time Louis MacNeice was much better. His appearance was hardly yet as should have been the mien of the most eminent poet present, but he was able to converse, a trifle diffidently, on general topics such as, my diary surprisingly records, Indian sculpture, a subject alien to the occasion.

About 2.30 p.m. a start was made for the graveyard at Drumcliffe four miles away. By this time a drenching mist was driving in from the Atlantic. Ben Bulben was wrapped in clouds; the scene became more desolate every moment. The Drumcliffe church was a stark nineteenth-century building. Nearby was the stump of a Round Tower, a survival from the same date as the Celtic cross adjacent to it. The open grave was by the church door. Its sides were lined with bracken and flowers, and it appeared unusually deep. The visiting notabilities stood assembled by it. One saw the Earl of Longford, so very stout compared to his brother, the present holder of the title. With him was the Countess, and nearby the handsome actor, Michael MacLiammoir, and Joseph Hone, my brother-in-law, a leading Dublin man of letters. De Valera, tall and severe, caught the eye. Other poets, dramatists and political figures were present, such as Erskine Childers, son of the patriot who had been on the wrong side at the wrong moment and was shot at dawn. I did not see Lord Dunsany. The service began; five clergymen took part. Autograph hunters, chiefly small boys, circulated with their notebooks. The feeling was not as solemn and dramatic as Yeats would have liked. Everyone was doing his best, but it was so wet that you had to keep your hat on or your umbrella up. Ben Bulben, the sacred mountain, the important bit of the scenery, remained shrouded. There seemed some difficulty in lowering the coffin into the deep grave. The Last Post was sounded and the crowd dispersed talking in groups. There was no trace of the bravado that ends the Yeats poem and is now on the tombstone:

> *Cast a cold eye*
> *On life, on death,*
> *Horseman, pass by.*

It remained for Louis MacNeice to say the final word. He declared that the wrong body had been buried. They had dug up at Menton the body of a Frenchman with a club foot. A mistake, but did it really matter? But was it certain he knew what he was talking about? Why, it's common knowledge in Menton, he assured us. Well, then, what do you think should be done? we asked. Can't do anything now, he said. Everyone then went back to the hotel for tea.

Years later in Maria Carras's[1] drawing-room in London I met Louis MacNeice again. We recalled how in 1948 we had driven together across Ireland to the famous funeral. He still insisted it was not Yeats's body that was buried.

Jack Yeats survived till 1957 when he was eighty-six. Of his last days Waddington wrote to me: 'Jack Yeats wanted to die. The last two years were spent in a nursing home. After the first year, when he found it impossible to go home, he knew that there

[1] Then the wife of the millionaire Greek shipowner.

would be no more painting. Gradually came a wearying. "There is nothing funny in the long hours spent in bed and in this room alone. I can no longer write very much, even a short letter. Sometimes even signing my name is a burden," he said. "I had painted every picture I had vowed to paint, yet still I am here." He retained his full faculties to the end; then quietly slipped away. Recognition had partly come.'

It was soon after writing me this letter that Waddington opened his gallery in Cork Street, W.I.

I should mention that in the course of one of my visits to Dublin in 1946 I came across Louis Le Brocquy. At that time he was unknown, not only in London, but even in his native city of Dublin. He had not been spotted by Victor Waddington, or if Waddington had cast an eye on him, it was a cold eye. I forget how it was that I found myself in his studio, a room on the first floor of a house just off Merrion Square. He showed me his pictures, both watercolours and oils. In them was represented the Ireland of his fancy, which was an original fancy. His style was much more *avant-garde* than Yeats's. They were both interpreting aspects of Irish life, Yeats as a romantic, Le Brocquy as a wanderer in secret by-ways. What I immediately saw was that his work would sell in London and make a sensation. There was no reason for him to remain isolated in Dublin a moment longer. I suggested to one of the directors of the Leicester Galleries who happened to be in Dublin, that he should pay Le Brocquy a visit. He did so and offered to exhibit in a London mixed show a few months later ten pen-and-wash drawings and four oil paintings. When this came on in October 1946 I wrote a review for the *Observer*. All his fourteen pictures had been bought immediately, a very unusual success for an unknown artist. I spoke of his mood, eerie and of some other world, inspired by his contemplation of the Mayo tinkers, 'wanderers closer to the earth and to the earth's old presences than any other class in Ireland. The figures flit by or stand startled, gaze down or sideways. There is always a secret, and there is silence and no invitation to break it. Nothing could be more different from the traditional Irishman.'

Le Brocquy was immediately taken up by Charles and Peter

Gimpel, who gave him a full exhibition in May 1947 which was successful. He was launched on the international market.

I remained art critic of the *Observer* during 1946 and 1947, when I ceased to contribute because my opinion of Sir Alfred Munnings differed from the editor's. I remained *Time & Tide*'s critic until 1951. From that date I no longer made the weekly round of the galleries and contributed to the press only occasionally and by special request. During the closing year of my time with *Time & Tide* there was a squabble between me and Eric Newton over which of us had first called Lowry an English master. I was asked by the Reid Lefevre Gallery to write for them a little book on Lowry, 12,000 words with 24 illustrations. Accordingly I visited him at his house in Manchester, where I stayed for a few days. The gallery provided me with copies of all the London reviews of his work from the time when he began to exhibit there in 1939. Some of the reviewers had little opinion of him and did not realize at first that he was an English original artist. That he was that great rarity was the theme of my little book.

Eric Newton, like Lowry a Manchester man, had before 1939 admired him as an interpreter of the industrial life of the Midlands, but did not write on him in the London press until his first exhibition with Reid Lefevre in 1939. In my volume I said I would have liked to have seen him praise Lowry more warmly. This put him out of humour. He disliked being told his business. He also found it odd that Reid Lefevre had not commissioned him to write the book.

I was astonished when I got his letters of protest. I had done nothing but record the plain facts as revealed in the press cuttings supplied me by Reid Lefevre. I wrote at once and begged him to forgive me if there was anything in my text which he found disagreeable. He replied that he did forgive me. He did not think much of the book, however, and had sent Reid Lefevre 'a full commentary on it, which I am sure he will show you'. They did not show it to me.

I mention this stupid altercation because it shows how careful I had to be as an outsider. Newton was an established critic before I came on the scene. Besides current criticism he had written several art books. The intrusion of an amateur like myself was not welcome. True, by this time I was over sixty, and had been contributing to the press on art in general for over ten years. Nevertheless, I was a junior and, as Wyndham Lewis had told me, should be more modest.

7

General Aung San, the Burmese national hero, in London

THOUGH BUSY ALL the forties with art criticism, I managed not to neglect my writing, which was my main happiness, and, after my pension, my main source of income. There is a famous picture by Kuo T'ai Chih (fourth century A.D.) in the British Museum, called the *Admonitions of the Instructress*. One of the admonitions was not to boast. Without incurring reproof, I can, I trust, state that during the forties I published eleven books with China and Burma as their theme. My official connection with Burma was severed, but it remained the chief source of my inspiration. What had happened there since I left in 1934 was dramatic in the extreme, invasion by the Japanese in 1942, rout of the Japanese in 1944-5, and in 1947 the end of British imperial rule and the founding of a Burmese republic. I have related at length in my *Last and First in Burma* (1956) how this came about. Here all I need say is that the arrival in London on 8th January 1947 of General Aung San, the Burmese national hero, with a delegation, in order to obtain the British Government's assent to the establishment of the Republic, was for me a moment of intense personal interest. It gave a meaning to my life. Since the thirties I had hoped that a Commonwealth government would eventuate; I did not foresee that the Burmese would be able to demand and obtain a republic. Things had moved so slowly in my time.

General Aung San, the chief protagonist in this capital event in Burmese history, was a man of only thirty, quietly resolute, not at all the flamboyant leader. He now put up at the Dorchester Hotel with his delegation. His chief adviser was U Tin Tut, an able man who had been till recently a member of the Indian Civil Service, from which he had resigned a short while before so as to be free to enter politics. I received a note from him on 27th January, after the negotiations with the Cabinet were over, inviting me to come to the Dorchester, so that he could introduce me to General Aung San. We had tea first, at which he told me that all General Aung San's demands had been granted. Burma was free to remain in the Commonwealth or become a republic, as she wished. An agreement had just been signed to that effect. He then took me to an adjoining room and introduced me. Aung San did not look like a man in a moment of triumph. His manner was shy, though blunt, retiring though severe. Some kind of inner excitement possessed him. When he spoke, it was in wonderment at his success, though, as he reminded me, it remained for him to convince the people when he got back to Burma that the paper he had signed did truly guarantee their liberation.

I was asked to stay on for an informal dinner which was served in the General's suite. The delegates, with the exception of one of their number, U Saw, sat down to it. Had U Saw come to dinner, we would have had sitting with us Aung San's implacable rival, who was secretly plotting to overthrow him. He was the person who nine years before had proposed my health at the dinner given me in Rangoon on my return from the Shan States. I had not seen him since. He was a most dangerous man.

In the course of dinner I asked Aung San, since the Cabinet had left him free to choose either Commonwealth or republican status, which of the two he preferred. His reply was that while he saw advantages in Commonwealth status, he believed the Burmese to be set on a Republic. When I asked him this question I did not know that Lord Mountbatten had asked him the same question when Aung San called on him in London a few days before. The answer he gave was more personal, for he had a warm regard for Lord Mountbatten, who as Supreme Commander S.E. Asia had befriended him, particularly in 1945, when a group of Rangoon senior officials advised that he be arrested and tried for treason. Mountbatten was aware that this was not the only attempt by British officialdom to get Aung San out of the way. In 1946 after he had left the East on the termination of his appointment as Supreme Commander, they sought to have Aung San arrested and tried for murder. This was quashed by Attlee. Aung San now told Mountbatten that had it not been for these two attempts to have him put to death, he would be more inclined to advise his supporters to choose Commonwealth status. But as it was, it would be useless for him to try and persuade them, their resentment being such that they were resolved to be rid of the British altogether.

Two days after I dined with him, Aung San gave a reception in the Dorchester to the Diplomatic Corps and Members of Parliament. My family and I attended. I found it most interesting to watch how this young man, who had never been to England before and whose social experience hardly extended beyond the usages of Burmese society, much less cosmopolitan then than now, received his guests as they were announced with pleasant assurance. A neat little figure in his uniform as General, he was eyed with some curiosity by the foreign diplomats, who addressed him as Your Excellency and did not hide their respect for the adroit way he had handled the negotiations with the British Cabinet. In this atmosphere of easy affability his habitual reserve thawed; he was genial and gay. It was as if for the first time he was conscious that he was not only the idol of the Burmese nation but an international celebrity.

The Dorchester itself, however, was not at its best. The central heating had broken down. The vast reception room was warmed only by a few scattered little electric fires. Everyone was wearing their overcoats. Outside midwinter reigned. The basin of the fountain in front of the main entrance was frozen hard. But the cold did not chill the high spirits of the Burmese on this great occasion. After the departure of the M.P.s and diplomats, the Burmese guests, mostly students resident in London at the time, demanded music. A Burmese band appeared from nowhere, and lively Burmese airs filled the hall. There was a piano in a corner, and Ma Than E, a clever cosmopolitan girl, called Matinée by her friends, who had come over from Hollywood, sat at it playing

Burmese tunes. Aung San seemed for the moment to forgo his role of Bogyok (the Lofty Captain) as he was called, and joined in the fun and singing, though remaining a little mysterious, as if not wholly unmindful of the prophecy which long ago had foretold his coming as deliverer.

It was no time for me to linger. Giving Aung San a copy with dedication of my new book, *Foreign Mud*, I bade him farewell, wishing him good fortune, the successful completion of his task, vain words for alas! in five months he lay dead in his council chamber, riddled by the bullets of U Saw's gunmen.

8

Topolski, Korda, Astor and the Princess Zeid

FEBRUARY WAS NO warmer than January 1947. The severe winter was made the harder to bear by the difficulty of getting enough coal. On 14th February I note: 'extreme cold continues'. On the 17th I managed to buy a bag of coke off the ration. In some respects the food and coal situation was harsher than during the war. On 18th February I have: 'lunched at Simpsons in the Strand. Only rabbit left.' That afternoon I met Arthur Waley in the London Library. 'He was hardly visible in the gloom. Candles in bottles.' On the 19th: 'Cold still intense, but coal merchant manages a small delivery.' I was working hard polishing up a new book, *The First Holy One*, a promenade into the Confucian background which when published in 1948 irritated Arthur Waley. On 4th March there was a deluge of snow. That was the prelude of a flood which drove us out of our house. Heavy snow continued for some days till the Cotswolds were buried to the depth of several feet. A sudden thaw set in on the 12th and the liquid snow was precipitated into the Thames, which by the 14th grew into a raging torrent. The Conservancy lost control of the river. It overflowed its banks and began to advance upon the low-lying part of Maidenhead where our house stood. Alarmed by the signs that a serious flood was on the way, I saw I must move the car from my garage to higher ground the first thing next day. But looking out of the window at 11 p.m. I was startled to perceive the water gushing into the garden. The car was trapped. At 8 a.m. next morning, the 15th, the water was at the top of the hall door steps, only an inch or so below the level of the floor inside. At midday it entered the house, bubbling up through the boards. By the afternoon it was eight inches deep on the ground floor. In a frantic hurry we carried all we could upstairs, such as books, the Persian rugs and part of my art collection. It was still possible to cook in the kitchen in waders. But by the next morning the gas failed. We decided to evacuate the house if we could. In the garden there were four feet of water; a strong current was sweeping down the road past the gate. The question was whether we could get out. The phone by now was dead. We had no boat. But Mr. Light, who lived next door, was within earshot. He had a small boat and promised to evacuate us after he had rowed his family to a friend's house on higher ground. His telephone had not yet failed and we asked him to ring Feliks Topolski in London, who out of good nature had telephoned the previous day to inquire how we were, when he read the news in the morning paper. 'Say we are evacuating and coming up to London at once,' we shouted, 'and ask him to book us rooms in some hotel.' This Mr. Light did and took his family off.

Time passed and we waited anxiously. At last we saw him put into his garden. He appeared exhausted and when we shouted, asking him to come and take us as soon as possible, for the water was still rising, he declared he must rest a moment and have a mouthful of food, for he had had a hard struggle getting back and at a corner had been nearly caught in a fierce current and swept into the Thames, where he'd have had no chance. After what seemed an age he rowed his boat to our door. There were four of us with suitcases, a dog and a cat. His boat was very small and, when we were packed in, was hardly more than two inches out of the water. It was going to be a delicate passage. We set out cautiously, Mr. Light punting with one oar by a safer route than the one which had so nearly been fatal for him. There were moments of danger but in ten minutes we were safely ashore, all except the cat, which got out of its basket and in a panic leapt up a tree we were passing and was never seen again.

Dry land seemed a delightful place, as delightful to feel under the feet as it does for shipwrecked seafarers landed by lifeboat. We got to the railway station and took the next train to London. Though we relied absolutely on Topolski finding a hotel, we felt forlorn when we got out at Paddington. We did not know what arrangements he had made. It was already late, past six o'clock. We must ring him at once. But the telephones we tried were out of order. We felt more like refugees than ever. At last I got a phone to work and heard Topolski's voice. It sounded to me like an angel's voice. 'All's arranged,' he said. 'I've managed to book you at the Esplanade Hotel, near us. I know the proprietor. He's a Pole. You'll be all right there. It's a comfortable place and he's promised to take you at a reduced rate. But come on to my house first and have supper. Marion is cooking it.' Much cheered we got a taxi.

After that all was well. We had a warm welcome, a splendid supper and were taken to the Esplanade, an unusually agreeable hostelry. We were thirteen days there waiting for news that the flood had subsided. We had an enjoyable time, were dry and well fed, and had plenty to do instead of being imprisoned in the house at Maidenhead. One was anxious about one's possessions, of course. Everything we owned had been abandoned. The police were warned to keep an eye, but thieves with a boat might well have ransacked the place.

My entry for 29th March is: 'Leave for Maidenhead by the 9.15 a.m. train. Arrive to find that the flood has completely drained back into the river. We could walk through the garden to the hall door steps. The house is in a hideous mess, but no damage has been done to its contents. We set to work to dry it with all the fires we possess.' The word *hideous* was not an overstatement. The water had been eighteen inches deep in the lower rooms and deposited a filthy slime on the carpets and a nasty mark on the wallpaper. There were drowned rats lying here and there. The legs of some of the marquetry furniture were peeling. However, everything valuable was in place. The bronze Buddhas dreamed on in the cabinets as if nothing had happened. In short, the damage was easily reparable. April 2nd: 'Still drying the house.' April 6th: 'Walls growing fungus.' April 16th: 'Walls still growing fungus.' But all in all my luck had held again.

The best piece of luck was having Topolski as a stand-by. He was now at the top of his reputation. I had known him since 1941. He had left Poland and come over to London in the middle thirties. In the early forties several books of his drawings were published with introductory texts by such well-known people as James Laver and Sir Stafford Cripps. In 1946 I had written the introduction for his *Three Continents*, a splendid selection of war drawings. As art critic for *Time & Tide* I also commented regularly on his work when it appeared in exhibitions. We had become close friends. I frequently dined with him at his house and studio. There were generally others there, for he had a wide circle of admirers, and on certain days held a sort of salon. 'He is the great illustrator of these times' declared the *Manchester Guardian*. The *Connoisseur* pronounced him the superior of Daumier and Guys. *La France Libre* compared his drawings to 'Le dance des nègres', and called them 'un jaillissement naturel'. One met in his studio or in his house such people as Ram Gopal, the Indian dancer, Prince Philip before he became Duke of Edinburgh, Krishna Menon, the Indian High Commissioner, Bertrand Russell, Bernard Shaw, Henry Moore, Augustus John, together with poets like Mervyn Peake, the Polish Count Tarnowski, Sir Francis Rose and a Royal Highness in the Princess Fahr-el-Nissa Zeid, wife of the Iraq Ambassador, besides politicians, actors, film and television people, composers and Russian dancers.

In this agreeable setting I had the advantage of meeting many notabilities of the day, especially advantageous as I had stage and film expectations. I had recently met Korda, who professed to see in my books and published plays likely material for his films; Robert Helpmann, at this time lessee of the Duchess Theatre, was eager to put on my play *Lord of the Three Worlds* with himself in the leading part. Mr. Dalrymple, an associate of Korda's, took an option on my *Land of the Great Image*. Stephen Mitchell, on the publication of my play *White of Mergen*, wired that he wanted to secure the rights immediately. A composer, Guirne Creith, was so attracted by my *Quest for Sita*, embellished by the best line drawings Mervyn Peake ever did, that she wrote a ballet on the theme, which interested the management of Sadlers Wells.

Guests at a party given by H.R.H. the Princess Zeid at the Iraq Embassy, 1949. Centre row: Lady Frederica Rose; Kathleen Raine; H.R.H.; John Hayward in bath chair speaking with Maurice Collis

That Robert Helpmann, a bewitching actor and dancer, saw himself captivating London in the part of the mad king in *Lord of the Three Worlds*[1] made me silly with joy. The king's type of hallucination exactly suited him, he declared. We lunched together. 'How I love the line—"he died ensorcelled",' he exclaimed; 'I could whisper it in a tone to make the house shudder.' But the Duchess Theatre was too small. To produce the play there was impossible and he had to abandon the idea, much to his chagrin. Guirne Creith's ballet on *Quest for Sita* failed in the end to satisfy the Sadlers Wells management, which wanted unacceptable amendments. Stephen Mitchell's boast that he was going to make *White of Mergen* into a second *Mutiny on the Bounty* never materialized. Mr. Dalrymple, though he paid me liberally for writing a film treatment for *The Land of the Great Image*, had finally to say it was a project beyond his means.

But with Korda it did look as if something material would eventuate. I was associated with him for quite a while and got to like him very much. He had a presence all his own, was such a cultivated lively man, a striking personality, extravagant, a showman, but a sort of genius. I had a lavish retaining fee. His premises were one of the huge buildings adjoining Apsley House at Hyde Park Corner. 'Come and have lunch in my private room,' he would say to me, 'a lap-lunch'. We would sit just the two of us there, a tray on the knee with appetizing things on it. The room was bright with his artist brother's pictures, painted in a post-impressionist style. Bookshelves lined the walls. He would take down a volume of Propertius or Horace, turn over the leaves and exclaim at some beauty. One day he would declare: 'I'll do *Siamese White.*' Another day it would be: 'I'd rather you wrote me something new, not hashed up out of your published books, a new story altogether, a strange wonderful eastern tale, something far away, impossible, mysterious, yet easy to understand.' So I wrote him *The Mystery of Dead Lovers*[2] on the theme of the Emperor Shah Jehan and Muntaz Mahal, with the Himālaya, the

[1] The edition published by Faber & Faber in 1946 had some eighty drawings by Topolski in his liveliest vein.

[2] Published in 1951 by Faber & Faber with illustrations by Cawthra Mulock.

Taj and a Maharishi thrown in. He liked it immensely, but now wanted me first to collaborate with his other brother, Zoltan, in projects which he planned to film immediately. Among these were scripts for Kipling's *Jungle Book* and Alan Paton's *Cry the Beloved Country*, a South African novel, a 1948 best seller. My retaining fee was increased. I was paid thousands of pounds. I collaborated with Zoltan, a hardworking patient fellow. *Cry the Beloved Country* I believe was filmed. But none of the other schemes came to anything.

One morning I went into Zoltan's room and found him engaged on a film script for Graham Greene's *Heart of the Matter*. 'The way it winds up won't do for the films,' said he. 'I've changed it, given the story a better ending.' I asked how Graham Greene liked that. 'Oh, he doesn't mind,' said Zoltan. 'Told me to improve it if I could.' Graham Greene and Korda were good friends. I remember once John Hayward telling me how fond Korda was of talking about old times in Hungary when he was a poet and when he was poor, and how one wet afternoon, when sitting over drinks with Graham Greene at Claridges and reminiscing about those happy carefree days, a sudden revulsion for London overcame him. He pressed a button and told the desk to charter a plane to take him and Greene at once to the Riviera.

Despite his reluctance to stick to a programme and get on with film production in a methodical manner, his name as the greatest film magnate was in everyone's mouth. He owed his popularity and reputation largely to his charm. Some American bosses, if equally extravagant, were less considerate. John Hayward repeated to me what Graham Greene once told him of Selznick. This American magnate wired from Hollywood to Greene in London asking him to come over at once for a talk. Greene, scenting a contract, flew over. He found Selznick sitting in his car. It was fitted with a wireless telephone on which he was talking at his ease to someone in London. Greene found it a bit queer that he hadn't thought of ringing instead of sending for him. It turned out too that he had no particular offer to make. Korda never treated authors like that.

My books, liked for a time by stage and film producers, were not in the end found suitable for that market. What merits they had did not add up to a popular success with audiences accustomed to traditional fare. It was just as well that I was not sucked into that world. The attractions were great, a lot of money was promised. But I might have been led away altogether from the sort of work I was best fitted to do and which had given me my reputation. It was, no doubt, a delightful distraction to meet the film and stage people and I was disappointed when, for all their promises, they could not manage to put my work on the stage or the screen. But I soon got over it and fell back on my proper line of writing, the wiser for the experience. I would only have got disgusted if I had continued to write otherwise.

The people I already knew in literary and art circles were more suited to my character and sufficed to keep me happy. I particularly recall the pleasure I got from a visit to Henry Moore in August 1947. It was a lovely summer day when I drove over to see him at his house, Hoglands, in the tiny village of Perry Green, near Much Hadham, in Hertfordshire, a drive of fifty miles or more from Maidenhead. He was already internationally known and had had monographs written on his sculpture by Herbert Read and by J. J. Sweeney, the American critic. But he was not even half-way to the eminence he has now reached. He could not sell his sculptures easily, and was largely dependent on commissions. He still kept his teaching job at the Chelsea Arts School because he could not afford to give up the regular salary it brought in, small though it was.

It is very interesting to meet a man of genius before he has been fully acclaimed by the world. At the date of my visit he was forty-nine years of age. Emerging from the country lanes on to the green where he lived, one saw a cottage with a tumbled roof, fields beyond, a rural corner like a Morland picture, not a setting one would expect for a revolutionary sculptor. Adjacent to the house was his studio. Before it on a terrace I saw three huge monoliths, which the chisel had touched just enough to stamp them with the hand of Henry Moore. Seen through greenery that partly screened them, the stones seemed to be taking the form of three presences, about to turn into the three fates or some such

subliminal personification. These scarce articulate shapes hinted at
a world much older than Morland's. One advanced on tiptoe and
presented oneself.

There was no trace of mystification, however, in Henry
Moore's appearance and manner, which were plain English. Indeed, his burly form would not have seemed out of place in a
Morland group. How came it that apparently so downright an
Englishman was turning stone into shapes which belonged to an
unseen and hitherto unexplored penumbra? That was what made
a visit to him in his retreat such an experience. A normal sort of
man was doing extraordinary things. Looking at his stone creatures you could not be sure whether you were looking at rocks or
at humanity or animality. There was a secret he was telling you
in his own language.

A visit to Henry Moore was a solemnity not elsewhere experienced, but there were occasions in congenial company when
memorable things were said. I remember being much delighted
by a remark I heard casually dropped at a party in Lady Kilmar-
nock's house by an amusing man, a portrait painter, named David
Roth. He said that Dreyfus became a bore in his old age. After
being adjudged a traitor in 1895, degraded from his rank in the
French army, deported to Devil's Island in French Guiana, in a
chain-gang there for ten years, brought back to France and in 1906,
acquitted after lengthy retrials which threw the entire French
nation into a frenzy of excitement, he was reinstated in the army
with the rank of major. With what result? He became a bore!
What better proof that he was innocent?

Going the round at this time I had other glimpses of rich
comedy. On 12th October 1948 I found myself seated at table
with Harold Nicolson in the Arts Dinner Club. He had not met
me before though he had been extremely generous in his reviews
of my books. In the course of the meal he told me some anecdotes
about Slatin Pasha, which to me were of especial interest as
Slatin's wife had suggested my writing his biography and proposed letting me have his papers. (In fact, this came to nothing.)
Nicolson said to me: 'Some years ago I was dining with Kitchener
and Slatin in Khartoum when Slatin pointed to a wall and de-

clared he had put up every stone of it while prisoner of the Khalifa, the Madhi's successor. He told how the Khalifa kept him chained by the foot to the palace door and would throw him bits of meat at meal times. He was porter, later mason, and finally a sort of adviser. Years passed and at last the British Secret Service engineered his escape, providing him with a dromedary for the 80 mile ride across the desert to Wadi Halfa on the Nile. After 40 miles the dromedary lay down and expired. "I had to walk" Slatin said "the rest of the way, a nightmare tramp. On the outskirts of Wadi Halfa, when challenged by the British sentries, I was so exhausted that I couldn't remember a word of English, and answered the sentry's questions in Arabic. I was taken into custody as a Dervish spy and had difficulty in establishing my identity." ' Harold Nicolson related this anecdote with amusing relish. It does not appear in the selections from his diary recently published by his son.

It was at this period that I first met H.R.H. the Princess Fahr-el-Nissa Zeid, whose parties at the Iraq Embassy were to be notable occasions. The Princess was Turkish by birth. She had first married the nephew of the Grand Vizier of Abdul Hamid, the last of the Caliphs. After the fall of the Caliphate, one result of which was the death of her husband, she married H.R.H. Prince Zeid el Hussein, by birth heir to the throne of Iraq, though on marrying her his claim as Crown Prince lapsed under the dynastic rules of the Hashemite dynasty, which forbade marriage to a foreigner. He became Iraq's Ambassador at the Court of St. James about 1947. I met the Princess first at an exhibition of her paintings in February 1948 at the St. George's Gallery in Grosvenor Street, the director of which was Madame Jaray, well known before the war in Vienna, where her art gallery was one of the best. The war obliged her to abandon it and come to London. When I walked into the gallery and saw what a good painter the Princess was, I asked to be introduced to her. That was the start of a long friendship.

Encouraged by the press notices she got for her St. George's exhibition, the Princess exhibited again the next year, this time at the Gimpel gallery, as the St. George's was too cramped for her largest pictures. My diary has this on the private view there: 'The occasion resembled a diplomatic reception without drinks. I spoke to the Princess's grand-nephew, King Faisal of Iraq, aged thirteen and a half and about to go to Harrow, a wonderfully self-possessed boy. The French Ambassador Monsieur Massigli was there, as were Lord Robert Crichton-Stuart, brother of the Marquis of Bute, Topolski and the Hon. Steven Runciman, the noted Byzantine historian, a friend of the Princess's from Turkish days. In short it was a more than usually distinguished private view. "Write and tell me what you think," the Princess whispered to me as I left.'

Ten days later she invited me to lunch with her at the Iraq Embassy, 15 Kensington Palace Gardens, popularly known as Millionaires' Row. The house had until recently been the young King of Iraq's residence. My diary has: 'I found her alone in her boudoir. She was dressed in black and looked remarkably young, though she must be 47 or so. No one else had been invited. Soon lunch was announced and we passed into the main dining room. An elaborate meal of lobster and turkey was served on solid silver plates. The Princess was animated. She spoke of her youth in Istanbul, of her first marriage and how she sought to gather about her the artists and writers of the capital. I suggested to her that she should start a salon in London, saying that she had all the personal qualifications, together with a fine large house. She liked the idea, but her experience told her it was not an easy thing to do successfully. When I left she made me a present of dates and wine with a lavish gesture.'

A few days later I ran into her at Mr. Messens's gallery, the London. 'What a lucky meeting!' she exclaimed, coming up. She assured me that she had been thinking over my suggestion to invite artists and writers to the embassy and had decided to do it. They would enliven the Prince's ambassadorial receptions.

Her first party was on 9th March 1949. I brought Merlyn Evans with me, an artist I admired, whom I thought she would like. Other notabilities there were John Hayward, Louis MacNeice, Kathleen Raine, the poetess, Louis Le Broquy, Steven Runciman, Richard Gainsborough, who had just founded his art magazine, Francis Rose and his wife Frederica, Rothenstein, director of the

Tate, and so on. There was plenty to drink. Everyone enjoyed themselves. The Princess was satisfied that she had made a fair start. Her press photographer took the picture given here, showing a corner in her salon with herself in a characteristically informal attitude among her guests. Her parties continued for the next nine years, her last one being in May 1958 on King Faisal's twenty-third birthday, shortly before his assassination and the massacre in Baghdad of all the members of the Iraq royal family except Prince Zeid, the Princess's husband, who was in London. The parties had got larger as time went on and more cosmopolitan. Politics, diplomacy, art, letters and society generally were cleverly mixed. The Princess grew to be a noted London hostess. The Prince was well suited by all this. His manner was endearing; he was naturally convivial, modest and easy. The Princess was always animated, yet imposing. She was the life and soul of every occasion. Her paintings were in a studio adjoining the salon and she allowed those interested to have a peep at them, a personal touch missing in the average embassy function.

My diary contains glimpses of these parties. Thus: 'The Princess Alice said she admired her hostess's painting, though it is difficult to perceive how she managed this, as she admitted to being a friend of Munnings. Among the guests was Tambimuttu, the Singalese poet, who wrote such good verse in English, that he was made editor of a London poetry magazine. On this occasion, much enlivened by the refreshments, he went up to the Princess Alice and said, in a tender way, that she had a marvellous skin. Her reply was that as she was old enough to be his grandmother she ought not to let such thoughts trouble him. When leaving the party he swayed on the hall door steps, but Mr Hooper, the butler, hastened up and supported him to a waiting taxi.'

At this party Steven Runciman came in accompanied by Giorgio de Chirico, just arrived from Italy for an exhibition of his pictures at the Royal Society of British Artists. Chirico was a man of medium height, with white hair and a pleasant expression. He was internationally famous for his surrealist paintings[1] as far back

[1] See the important place Wilenski gives him in his *Modern French Painting* (1940).

as 1914, but had come to regard his surrealism as an aberration and, representing himself as the prodigal son, returned to his early romantic style. Now in 1949 he was sixty-one. His London exhibition was to be confined to this post-surrealist work, none of which had been seen in England. His negation of the whole modern movement, in which he had been a leading protagonist, made him the most talked of artist at the moment. When Runciman introduced him to me, he said, as if to anticipate adverse criticism: 'Picasso has changed his style, and more than once. Why should it be laid to my charge that I have done the same?' I replied that we were not prejudiced here. He would be judged by the quality of his paintings. 'They are excellent,' he assured me.

The R.B.A. gave a lunch for him the following day. The Princess was assigned the seat beside him. In conversation with him after lunch in the room where a hundred of his paintings were on view, he had the look of a man who for a lifetime had painted at the centre of European art and crossed swords with the Parisian pundits. There was something tired, a trifle blasé and disillusioned in his air, as if he had heard what was now being said to him many times before and found it, though well meant, mostly cliché.

He and his wife asked me to a *tête-à-tête* lunch with them a few days later at the Pastoria in Leicester Square. He wished to thank me for writing a favourable leading article on his exhibition in Gainsborough's new art paper, then called *Art News & Review*. I found his mood more modest than at the R.B.A. luncheon. I noted, however, in my diary: 'Chirico is not a very easy person to talk to and his Russian wife is rather rigid. But I liked them. They asked me to come and see them in Rome and to promise to write to them.' But nothing came of this. Chirico on the whole was disappointed with his London exhibition. He felt that the R.B.A. gallery was a bad choice. A more select exhibition in a first-class West End gallery would have been the proper line for the celebrity that he undoubtedly was. His paintings have not been seen in London since.

During the nine years that Prince Zeid remained Iraq's ambassador in London, the Princess exhibited three times, twice as already noted and the third time at the Institute of Contemporary

Art at Roland Penrose's invitation. The party she gave in the Institute was more luxurious than any hitherto held there or seen since. She also exhibited in New York, Brussels and Paris. I have a note which suggests how happy she was made by the applause of Paris. 'When I called by appointment on the Princess Fahr-el-Nissa Zeid at the embassy, I was ushered by Mr Hooper, the butler, into the salon, where the refreshments which she invariably had ready for visitors, were displayed on a small table conveniently within reach. "Her Royal Highness will be down in a moment," said Mr Hooper as he poured me out a generous glass of whisky. A few minutes later the Princess entered. She complained of fatigue and was less ebullient than usual. I had brought her a trifling present, a small bronze weight in the form of a fabulous lion, a Burmese antiquity. She was immediately delighted, admired the little thing, and declared that she would turn it into a seal by having engraved on its flat base her name in Persian characters. She then blamed the butler for having poured me so small a whisky and demanded to know where her box of chocolates was. "Under the sofa, in its usual place, Your Royal Highness," said Mr Hooper, going down on a knee and fetching it out. After these preliminaries and when I had had a slice of smoked salmon, she opened her bag and took out a sheaf of press cuttings on her Paris exhibition and invited me to look at them. Her fatigue had disappeared, her normal high spirits were rising. Reading here and there I perceived that she had had an excellent reception. The French liked her style and enjoyed the idea of her being an oriental princess. She had evidently been very happy there and felt she had had an artistic success. She is not a woman given to understatement, which after all is a tedious trick, and eagerly kept drawing my attention to the best bits. To sit on the sofa and listen to her cries of delight as she pressed me to read was a simple pleasure as enjoyable for me as for her.'

During the fifties the Princess continued to add to her reputation in England and abroad. No artist can get established fully in nine years, but she was on the way to a substantial recognition of her talents. The catastrophe already alluded to ended her career as a hostess and a painter in London. In the embassy party of 2nd

May 1958, given to celebrate King Faisal's twenty-third birthday, all was as usual. There was not the smallest fear of any bad turn of events in Iraq. Yet two months later the young king was dead, and all his relations. The revolutionary government of Iraq relieved the Prince of his post as ambassador.

As soon as I heard the news I went round to the embassy to inquire. After the party of 2nd May the Princess had left for her country house on Ischia in the Bay of Naples. I did not expect to find her at the embassy but hoped to get news of her there. I had with me a letter which I intended to ask the embassy people to send on to her. My diary has: 'As I approached the building I saw that the curtains were drawn. It had a deserted air. On ringing the bell the door was opened by Mr Hooper, the butler I have got to know so well. He was neatly dressed in a black alpaca coat and white shirt. His big eyes looked very solemn in his florid face. I produced the letter which he promised to have forwarded to Ischia where it was believed the Princess was in residence. I did not ask where the Prince was, as I did not want to appear inquisitive. When the butler saw that I had not come to question him (for no doubt he had his instructions to keep his mouth shut), he began to linger and talk a little. It was impossible to foresee, he said, what their Royal Highnesses would now do. Whether they would take a house in London he did not know. "What a thing to happen in the 20th century!" he sighed. It was evident that he was grievously upset. Would the new government take him on or what? The catastrophe had come without warning, though I now recalled that the Prince in speaking to me had once dropped hints of his dissatisfaction with the Regent, Abdul Illah's, policy. He had thought it prudent to sell his real estate in Baghdad and invest in European securities. I said goodbye to Mr Hooper and left, certain, alas, that the Princess's reign as London hostess was over. The many hundreds of people who had enjoyed her parties knew they would never see the like again. There was no other woman in English society who could take the place of this Turkish Highness.'

9

Stanley Spencer, Scottie Wilson
and Mervyn Peake

I AM OBLIGED NOW to return to the date where I began to narrate
the Princess Fahr-el-Nissa's part in London society. There were,
of course, many other receptions of interest. I remember in particular one given by the Polish Ambassador, Mr. Michalowski, on
the centenary of the day when Chopin played before Queen
Victoria in 1849. The pianist Szpinalski was engaged, the programme ending with the celebrated Scherzo in C sharp minor,
op. 39. A letter of Chopin's has the following: 'Her Majesty was
very kind and spoke to me twice. Prince Albert drew near the
piano, a great favour, as they tell me.'

When Mr. Szpinalski had done his best, the audience was
invited downstairs to a buffet. 'On my way down,' I noted, 'the
Baroness Budberg, Korda's friend, whispered to me: "If there's
any vodka, for God's sake keep me some!" Everyone was pushing
to get down to the refreshments. There was no vodka however,
but plenty of whisky.'

At the party I was introduced to the Chinese Ambassador,
Cheng Tien-hsi, who appeared very pleased to speak to me. My
book *The First Holy One* was recently out, the book on Con-
fucianism which had irritated Arthur Waley. The Chinese Ambassador had read it and now said that he liked it so much that he
made a rule of reading passages from it to lecture audiences. I
record: 'He went on in a most animated manner, quoting the
Chinese poets on friendship and speaking of God. He was a little
drunk. At midnight he asked me to come back with him to the

Chinese embassy. We sat down in the dining room, which was laid for breakfast. He sent for Napoleon brandy and Chinese caviar. A special tea was made by the butler. "I don't want to sound vulgar," said he, "but I must tell you that the price of it is £6 a pound. It comes from the hills beyond my home." It had a subtle aroma and was a wonderful stimulant, easy on the stomach. We sat talking till 1 a.m. The brandy was finished and many cups of tea. He was uproariously happy, shouting and laughing. In all my life I have never had exactly such an experience. An ambassador, on first meeting, takes me to his house in the middle of the night and there, as if speaking to an old friend, pours out his thoughts. It was modelled, I suppose, on the traditional Chinese way two scholars should carouse together. When I said: "The Chinese surpass all nations because they know how to treat men of letters" he was profoundly pleased; I had caught the point.'

Besides such fantastical excursions into diplomatic society, I entered the fringe of a far more fantastic personality's life. On 17th July 1949 my diary records that the two Roses and Richard Gainsborough, mentioned as guests of the Princess Zeid's, came to visit me at Maidenhead and that I took them on to see Stanley Spencer. 'Spencer has a small house outside Cookham, called Cliveden View, because from its upper windows Lord Astor's Cliveden is visible. It is a squalid little place, furnished very cheaply and without even the minor comfort of electric light. We went upstairs to his studio, a small room with a hard bed in it and green oilcloth on the floor. Covering the whole of one wall was half of a huge unfinished painting.' This was one of the 'Glasgow Resurrections' on which he was engaged at the moment, his most tremendous compositions, later the subject of a monograph by Wilenski. 'Spencer also unrolled for us the other half of the picture and spread it out on the floor.' He displayed these paintings, now held to be his greatest creation, with an animated frank air which was without any consciousness of his celebrity.

At this date he was sixty and about to enter upon a period of prosperity. 'After showing us his paintings he took us downstairs where tea was ready, consisting of thick slices of bread with butter and honey. During tea he discoursed on his paintings, summing up by saying "I paint in the way that comes natural to me, and so can't help doing a lot of things which painting is nowadays supposed not to do, such as telling a story".'

We were much impressed by what we saw, particularly Spencer's masterly composition.

Before we left he said he would like to visit me and have a look at my art collection. On 14th August he came to tea and stayed three and a half hours talking about his art. He claimed there was a transcendental meaning behind the scenes he depicted and attempted to explain what that was. He talked on and on, but it was not possible to make out what he sought to convey. I have: 'He talked so much that he tired me somewhat. As I drove him home to Cookham, he said "I am miserably poor." '

At that time he was living chiefly on a weekly allowance of £3 paid him by Dudley Tooth, the Bruton Street dealer who for years had exhibited him. His great pictures were very difficult to sell, though soon after this Tooth raised his money to £10 a week.

I made another visit to his studio in August, accompanied by Topolski. On this occasion he produced what he called the Scrapbooks, which contained 120 of his drawings, works of special interest later bought by Lord Astor on my advice. These drawings had to do with four women. Spencer attached so much importance to them that though he at first let Topolski buy one, he changed his mind and demanded the drawing back. We had some notion of an erotic background, as of some secret life, but had little notion what it was. In short, we did not understand Spencer's art at all, though the Scrapbooks had explanatory notes.

My diary contains occasional further references to him at this time. I got to know him better, but was as far away as ever from grasping the significance of his *œuvre*. Though he talked unendingly about his pictures, I never could quite follow what he said. There were some people who claimed they could, but if you listened to their explanations you were no wiser.

Visitors who came down to see me at Maidenhead often asked to be taken to his studio. One occasion remains particularly in my memory, when I took Hamid Said, an Egyptian artist, accompanied by his wife Anne, an Englishwoman. They looked up to

Spencer as a mystic, and gazed earnestly at a huge resurrection painting of his. Spencer was in an impish mood, and talked more lightly of the picture than the Saids thought fitting. Their admiration amused him, for the picture's meaning was quite other than they supposed. He then tried to explain its significance, but though they listened with respect they could make no more of his explanation than I could. When the Saids had departed, thanking him for an experience they would always cherish, I took him for a drink. After one or two, he dropped his rigmarole and told two amusing stories about himself, which showed the pleasure he got from depicting himself as a victim. 'One day,' he said, 'Dudley Tooth asked me to call at his gallery in Bruton Street. I arrived with canvases under my arm, but the attendant at the door would not let me in. "We don't want any more today," said he, pointing to the pictures I was carrying. He thought I was a down and out artist, I suppose, hawking his paintings round. If it hadn't been that Dudley caught sight of me, I'd have been turned away.' The other story was of a similar sort, in which he is mistaken for a hungry gate-crasher. 'A publisher asked me to lunch at a Chinese restaurant in Soho. When I got there the fellow at the door extended his arms to block my way. "Go back!" he said. I tried to explain but was hustled into the street. On the pavement I stood near the window, hoping to catch a glimpse of my host. But the doorkeeper was watching. "No loitering!" he shouted. "Move on out of this!" It was pure luck that my friend came out to look for me.'

There was another well-known artist at this time who also did not look the part. Scottie Wilson could get first-class West End galleries like the Gimpels to exhibit his pictures, which sold at about £25. But he had other methods of raising money when he was short and in a hurry. Under date 29th June 1950 I have: 'Found Scottie Wilson selling his pictures in Sloane Square by the subway leading down to the Gents. "I'm selling them at a pound each" said he. That was a chance and I bought one called *The Indian Temple*, an excellent example of his unique style. The Gimpels, who have his pictures in stock, naturally do not like being undercut. But when the fancy takes him he sells off in this way. He is a strongly built little man, with huge fists and the face of a small East End dealer in odds and ends, except for his eyes which have a strange depth. In an accent partly Cockney and partly Scotch he told me he painted in the small hours, when he would fall into a sort of trance, and work without knowing what the subject was. I promised to write something for him to use as an introduction to an illustrated booklet he hoped to bring out.'

Six months later I attended the private view of his exhibition at the Gimpels. His paintings were being much admired by the critics. Somebody told me the Tate was buying one. My diary has: 'I asked Scottie about this, but he was not quite clear. In a vague way he said: "There was a man a while ago here with big glasses and a face like a Chinaman. Could that have been the Director of the Tate?" ' But he knew that the Arts Council was interested. His difficulty was to look like and behave like a West End artist. Messens, the director of the then London Gallery, who knew and admired Scottie's work, told me the following: 'One day Scottie appeared at the gallery and asked me for two pounds. Well aware that he lived from hand to mouth and probably hadn't on him the price of a meal, I passed him the notes at once. He then took from his pocket a roll of notes, not less than twenty I should say, added the two pounds to the roll and walked out. I do not understand the meaning of this.' It would be hard to tell exactly what Scottie was up to. Stanley Spencer used to drop in on Dudley Tooth and ask for something to go on with, but he did not as a rule ask for as much as two pounds, and never had a roll of twenty pounds in his life.

Another strange and gifted personality was Mervyn Peake, as poor as Spencer and as mysterious. His *Gormenghast*, the second volume of his now widely acclaimed trilogy, had come out in 1951. It was given a ferocious review by Michael Sadleir, but the Royal Society of Literature took another line. In a letter to me dated 6th May 1951 he wrote: 'Have you by any chance heard my good news? *Gormenghast* has been awarded the Heinemann Prize for literature for 1950 by the Royal Society of Literature and fills my trouser pockets to the tune of £100. Whereas I was lukewarm to any society, especially to any that began with "Royal", I now find that I am almost mawkish in my admiration for anything of that kind. I wonder why.'

In a second letter dated 15th June he wrote: 'Would you like to come for the Prize-Giving?—I shall be wearing my Eton collar. I am enclosing a card in case you feel like seeing me look bashful.' How to receive and pocket the envelope containing the cheque for £100 would require practice, he said. 'At what moment to start the upswing of the furtive forearm? Whether to look like a sick eagle as one misses one's footing and collides with the potted palm.' The letter ends with a lively drawing of himself reaching for the envelope and kicking over the palm.

The prize-giving was on 26th June. My diary gives this account: 'After tea with Mervyn Peake and Maeve, his wife, I went on with them to the R.S. of Literature's rooms at 1 Hyde Park Gardens. I do not care for gatherings of this sort, but went to support Peake, whose *Gormenghast* is a masterpiece, and who is an extraordinary character himself, poet, painter and master of prose. The first person we met to speak to was Eddie Marsh, now in his 80th year at the tired end of a life spent as adjutant to eminent persons. Rab Butler was in the chair, not yet fifty but Chancellor of the Exchequer. His speech introducing Peake was not as good as the way he introduced the Budget. He admitted having only looked at *Gormenghast* for the first time that afternoon. No doubt he meant well, but managed to give the impression that it was not his cup of tea. As Peake's fervent admirers, we were indignant, silly of us, since the Society had chosen *Gormenghast* as the literary event of the year and so the chairman's speech did no harm. A lecture on Humanism followed. It dragged badly. Mervyn, however, endured the proceedings with amiability, every now and then feeling the lovely cheque in his trouser pocket.'

10

Visits to Italy

Since leaving the East in 1934 I had not been as far as Italy on the continent of Europe and was quite ignorant of the effect its architecture would have. Books are all very well, but descriptions and photographs give a limited impression of the presence of a great classical building. So in 1950 I decided on a tour to Tuscany, though at sixty-one years of age I was perhaps too old to feel as vividly as I might have felt earlier.

I was fortunate to have someone to accompany me whose sensibility would quicken my own. My daughter, Louise, was twenty-five years of age and was shortly to publish her first novel, *Without a Voice*. After reading it in proof I described in my diary the impact it made on me. 'It is a tender, subtle, poetical story, perfectly constructed and round, full of vivacity and insight. What a delightful thing it is that she should have achieved this! I could never have managed such a piece of character writing, for I must have the constant support of action and bold or curious drama. She can make do with small scenes and by the simplest means tells all she wants to tell. The episodes are woven into each other so deftly, that there is no noise or clatter. All goes softly and you are lifted to the end as if riding in a Bentley.'

So in April 1950 we set off together. I wrote an account of the tour immediately on return in May, which has not been published. A few citations from it will show the sort of things that struck us most.

Arrived at Siena, on our first walk into the town 'suddenly we saw the steps leading down into the Campo. The first sight of this famous piazza is exceedingly astonishing. It is in the form of a semi-circle, and much like what it was in the time of Dante who mentions it in his colloquy with the damned Salvani, former lord of Siena, who, pretending once to be a beggar, collected money in the Campo to ransom a friend.

> Quando vivea piu glorioso, disse,
> Liberamente nel campo di Siena,
> Ogni vergogna deposta, s'affisse.
> (Purgatorio Canto XI)'

What most delighted me in the Siena cathedral nearby was 'the pavement of 64 pictures in tarsia incised on slabs of white marble, the incisions filled with black cement. To prevent them being worn down by the feet of congregations they are kept covered by boards, but it happened that when we were there workmen were engaged in waxing them. I have never seen anything that pleased me more.'

At the church of San Domenico near the Cathedral we had a glimpse quite out of our period. Priests were conducting a service and one of them opened a golden reliquary on the altar. The interior was lit by electric light and a head was visible in it. We learned it was the mummified head of St. Catherine, the patron saint of Siena. The city at some period had been permitted by the Pope to cut it off the body which is preserved in Rome.

In Assisi we came on another relic of the sort in a crypt of the basilica built over the remains of Santa Chiara. Lying on top of her tomb behind a grille was her mummified body. The face, hands and feet were bare and black. The body, which had lain in the tomb for 500 years, was taken out in the eighteenth century and exposed to view. It was a very great attraction and source of revenue.

A fresco by Giotto in the upper church of San Francesco at Assisi I found strangely captivating. It commemorated the tender moment when St. Francis, who is shown constructing a manger for the Christmas festival, found the infant Christ in his arms.

In striking contrast was what we saw in the church of San Agostino in San Gimignano. We were looking at the Gozzoli frescoes behind the altar, when the door into the sacristy opened and we were invited by an old Augustinian monk with a great show of friendliness to enter and look round. Gothic cloisters enclosed a secluded garden, where the chanting of the choristers in the body of the church was muted. Unexpectedly the monk flung open a side door. We were astonished to behold within colossal figures of Mickey Mouse, Donald Duck and Pluto mounted on cardboard horses. The sacristan, who had told us already that he was eighty-nine years old and had seen Queen Victoria when she visited San Gimignano, displayed these effigies with simple pride. They were taken out for carnival processions, he said. He showed us also an enormous painted head of a girl and, working a lever, made her wink at us. To one side was an amiable sheep with spectacles. In his happy way, our guide went up to the cardboard horse on which Pluto was mounted, and tapping it over the muzzle with his stick, cried: 'Why, he doesn't know any more Italian than you do!' He was a tiny little man, very bent, but smiling and spritely. He led us back into the church, where he gently drew our attention to the offertory box.

One would have thought that an old monk, his life spent among mummified saints, was not the sort to have been so proud of ridiculous effigies suited to the taste of the modern proletariat. Their special attraction for him, however, lay in the fact that they were modern. The inhabitants of San Gimignano, no longer the feudal class for whom 700 years before the towers and palazzos of the town had been built, but small tradesmen and farmers, found novelties from abroad delightful. The palazzos had become tenements or flats, the towers derelict. Their architecture was splendid, but they were dreary places for twentieth-century townsmen. That Donald Duck, Mickey Mouse and Pluto were carefully stored in a room off sacred precincts where mummies of saints were adored, hinted at the secret longings of the people. A fresh breeze was blowing in, of which the old monk, too, had caught a refreshing whiff.

For the tourist these old Italian towns are wonderful to look at, but they would be suffocating to live in. Architecture is the most powerful of the arts; to have to live in its grip can alarm. Yet when we saw Pisa, the Campo there with the Leaning Tower, the Cathedral and the Baptistry, we felt their beauty to be so potent that it liberated rather than confined. I noted: 'As you look across the open Campo where stand the three masterpieces, the Leaning Tower, the Cathedral and the Baptistry, it is the last that most compels the eye. The white marble form can be compared to the papal crown; it is the most exquisite thing I have ever seen. It seems to float over the flat, and though very large and strong seems as airy as lace. To its external beauty are added acoustic marvels. The architecture becomes vibrant; it enchants both eye and ear. Inside the magic octagon was a man engaged to demonstrate its properties. He intoned four or five notes and these, caught up in the dome, were transformed into a chord, which resounded through the building with enormous volume. When the chord died away, the man clapped his hands and the echo sounded as if a multitude of people were applauding. A child who came in at this moment was tempted to sing and its treble was thrown back from the dome like the chant of a full choir. Surely the Baptistry at Pisa is the most mysterious building in the world. A modern architect might aspire to copy its formal beauty, but he could not even try to create the echo; the secret of it is known only to the old building and it will not impart it.'

The first Italian tour allowed of such teasing reflections. Going again in the spring of the next year (1951) we made straight for Rome. I had brushed up my Latin and read as much as I could before starting.

Rome is full of curiosities. The Popes' admiration for classical art was supplemented by their determination to adapt it to Catholic uses. In the centre of the magnificent piazza in front of St. Peter's is an Egyptian obelisk, which was brought from Heliopolis by Caligula and which Nero put in his circus near the future site of St. Peter's. In 1586 Pope Sixtus V admired it so much that he decided to make it the centre point of the San Pietro piazza. That meant moving it about half a mile, no easy task as the obelisk was a granite shaft eighty-three feet high of immense weight. With great difficulty it was lowered by cranes on to a vast waggon and dragged by 150 horses and 800 men to the new site. As it was a pagan idol inhabited by a devil, it had first to be exorcized. The evil spirit was no other than Julius Caesar himself, for the Romans had placed his ashes in a bronze globe on the top of the obelisk. Besides ejecting Divus Julius, other precautions had also to be taken. A High Mass was held in St. Peter's and the workmen were assembled and blessed. It was further thought essential to forbid them to speak during their task. For this prohibition magical reasons existed, though what precisely they were is not on record. In spite of its tenor, the inscription on the shaft was not effaced: 'Divo Caes Divi Julii F Augusti Ti Caesari Divi Aug F Augusta Sacrum', indicating that the obelisk was originally dedicated to the divine Emperors Augustus and Tiberius. Sixtus V considered that the removal of the globe from the top containing Julius Caesar's ashes and the substitution of a cross for the globe, together with an inscription beginning Ecce Crux Domini, sufficed to consecrate the pagan idol. To draw the populace's attention to the new dedication, an Indulgence for ten years was granted to all who, passing the monument, adored the cross on the top, provided that they repeated the Pater Noster. The engineer in charge of the removal was raised to the nobility and made a Knight of the Holy Spear, the spear which had pierced Christ's side and which was among the papal collection of relics. He was also presented with a large sum of money. Poems declaring the planting of the obelisk in front of St. Peter's to be a triumph of the Cross over paganism were composed, and distributed throughout Europe in translations.

This plain recital of how St. Peter's Needle, as it was called, came to be where it is, is so fantastical as to seem more myth than reality. Yet it is wonderfully informative. Properly understood it throws a flood of light on the relationship between classical and papal art. The two dovetailed into each other. As I began to realize this, I gazed with stupefaction at the obelisk whose metamorphoses had been achieved by words. Words had driven the evil spirits out of the stone, and words established it as a Christian monument. There was nothing incompatible between early and late Roman art. The same forms suited both. It was only necessary to change the nomenclature.

This discovery enabled us to take a more intelligent view of what we saw as we walked over Rome. The Pantheon, for instance, built about 30 B.C., has survived unchanged. It began by being the most important temple in the Roman metropolis. About A.D. 600 after the extinction of the Roman cult it was dedicated to the Virgin. A fifteenth-century guide-book,[1] written for the use of pilgrims, states that it had become essential to turn it into a Christian church because the evil spirits that abode in it were dangerous to passers-by, who often had seizures and fell insensible in the street. After its consecration, the images of the old gods were replaced by Christian images. No attempt, however, was made to alter the building. Even the inscription on the architrave: 'M Agrippa L F Cos Tertium Fecit' remains to this day. My impression of the Pantheon was that it expressed the might of classical Rome more forcibly than any other building in the city. By a change of nomenclature it was made to express the might of the papal church. The architecture, however, still gave off its original message, the power of classical Rome, for that was the emotion that inspired the architect.

It was this jumble of 2,000 years of meanings that entranced me in Rome. One was wandering in a fairyland. In St. Peter's, a Renaissance building, new birth of the classic, one stood under Michelangelo's dome, like the Pantheon's, and remarking the four massive piers supporting it, was delighted to know that in them were the four great relics, the Lance of St. Longinus, the head of St. Andrew, the bit of the True Cross brought back from Palestine by the Empress Helena and the napkin of St. Veronica. The last was an extraordinary curiosity. The mere sight of it gave indulgence from penance for the rest of your life.

Curious to relate the English have a niche in this fantastic necrology. Under a sculpture by Canova, one reads the names of James III, the Old Pretender, Bonnie Prince Charlie, the Young Pretender, and the latter's brother, the Cardinal Henry. The thought that in the whirligig of history a Roman Cardinal might have succeeded to the throne of England, gives one pause! The cost of the Canova monument was heavy, but Pope Pius VII paid

[1] *Mirabilia Urbis Romanae.* Edited and translated in 1889 by F. M. Nichols.

it. The story goes that George IV was asked to pay. But all his money had gone on the Brighton Pavilion. In the crypt below, among many other curious relics of the original St. Peter's, was the sarcophagus of Nicholas Breakspear. He began life as a beggar boy in the slums of London, rose to be a barrow boy with apples and somehow contrived to rise and rise until, as Adrian IV, he became the first English Pope, and so far the last. He must have been a man of remarkably solid attainments, but two small post-humous details make one feel he was an eccentric. On his red granite sarcophagus in the crypt are Medusa heads carved in relief. And when for some reason it was opened in 1600, his mummy was found wearing red Turkish slippers. If that is a fact, how illuminating it is! When you can relish its overtones, no need to pursue further your studies at Rome!

But we had not come to Italy to loiter among such fancies and savour delightful absurdities, but to catch if we could the authentic voice of the Eternal City. We heard the august tones before we left. During his rule Mussolini put together the fragments of the lost Ara Pacis, which were discovered set into palace walls and even built into drains, and housed them in a building he erected for the purpose. We came on this building unexpectedly and saw on its outer wall a long inscription which we were just sufficiently erudite to recognize as Augustus's autobiography, the famous Res Gestae which records with lapidary abruptness his consolidation of the empire whose foundation was laid by Julius Caesar. The inscription mentions the erection of the Ara Pacis by decree of the Senate, whose consecration was attended by the magistracy, the priests of the imperial cult and the Vestal Virgins. On entering the building housing the altar, we found that the reliefs in the form of a frieze that flanked it were of extraordinary quality. They depict the procession of the Roman magnates on their way to the consecration ceremony on 4th July 13 B.C. They struck me as the greatest work of art produced by imperial Rome. The procession is led by Augustus himself, walking with his son Tiberius, some thirty other grandees following, including the wives and children of the Julian family, all of them portraits. A most charming glimpse is given of high Roman society. Very dignified, their togas elegantly draped, the Patricians walk slowly, genially chatting, with an air of ease and polite aloofness, a consciousness of rank worn without offence.

To come from the phantasmagoria of papal Rome to this peep at the Roman gentry, the senatus populusque Romanus, at a great moment in their history, was a profound illumination. We were face to face with the people whose literature, after two millenniums, we still cannot do without. It was in the hope of getting this glimpse through art that we had come to Rome. What had captivated the fancy, now was seen for what it was worth. The frieze of the Ara Pacis revealed a reality. We had come out of the fairyland of such places as the Lateran cloisters, where were the porphyry slab on which the soldiers cast lots for the Seamless Vesture, the columns rent by the earthquake at the moment of the Crucifixion, the wall on which the height of Jesus was marked, and the hole in the stone made by the wafer that fell from the paralysed hand of a priest who doubted the Real Presence. That wonderland we had greatly enjoyed. But now at last the Ara Pacis restored our reason.

I I

Anecdotes of notabilities met
in London

ON RETURN FROM Rome I resumed my normal round, work at home on some book, at the moment a volume of memoirs, and twice a week a trip to London by car to see friends and keep abreast. A few extracts from my diary will show what I used to come across.

In 1951 Feliks Topolski's studio was on the canal near Paddington. I was talking to him there when a yacht moored outside his window. 'He looked out and the owner, a tall lanky man, asked to be allowed to put a hosepipe on to a tap to fill his water tank. Topolski said he could and the man came in, fixed the pipe, and introduced himself as the Labour peer, Lord St Davids. When his tank was full he invited us aboard the yacht. He said it was his town residence, as he had given up his flat and kept on only his country house in Wales. "I move about the canals," he explained, "keeping conveniently close to the House of Lords when it's in session." As we were boarding the yacht, a shower of stones fell, flung by a troop of boys behind a wall on the other side of the canal. As the boys went on pelting the yacht, Feliks thought he had better phone the police. A mild constable arrived; the boys stopped. After giving us a drink Lord St Davids shoved off. "Sailing on the London canals is quite a high seas adventure," said he cheerfully. "The boys—good as savages." '

Sir Francis Rose and his wife Frederica lived in Flood Street. One evening when I was there a little party was on. 'Topolski was the first to arrive, followed shortly by John Davenport, whom

Frederica was not expecting. When somebody said he was on the stairs, she hastily hid the gin bottle in her bedroom; in the past he had so often drunk her last drop. He lived in the flat above. One day, she told me afterwards, "he came down rather drunk, rang our bell and hit Francis when he opened the door. Francis fell and seemed stunned. Alarmed what Davenport might do next I rang for the police. Before they arrived, however, Francis came to and made it up with Davenport." On the present occasion he was very agreeable. He had read *Siamese White* and wondered whether he could be a descendant of the Davenport who is one of the main characters in the book. By appearance a youngish thickset man, with protruding eyes, a bush of hair and a bright face, he was a striking and clever personality.'

I have a note of the day when Marion Topolski asked me to go with her to the National Gallery to see the director, Sir Philip Hendy, and ask him whether a picture they had bought was by Desiderio. We set out, she driving behind in her car with the picture. 'When I reached the gallery there was no sign of her. As I waited on the pavement I saw John Rothenstein. He gave me a casual salutation. On my explaining I was waiting for Marion Topolski and that we wanted to consult Hendy about a Desiderio, he said: "Oh, but I am taking him out," and with that disappeared into the building. I went on waiting and at last saw Marion hastening towards me. "Held up in a traffic jam" she said panting. At this moment Hendy was seen coming out with Rothenstein and Sir John Ridley, chairman of the Tate council. We rushed up and caught them when about to enter a car at the kerb. Marion had the Desiderio in her hand and explained. It was hardly a moment to ask for an expert opinion, but Hendy didn't mind. As he got into the car he glanced over his shoulder at the picture in an elegant manner which went well with his handsome face and said: "That is not a Desiderio" and added: "Take it in and ask Martin-James if you like." Accordingly we rang the bell at the private door and were admitted. By this time, however, we were in such a flurry that we could not remember the name he had mentioned. The porter, an agreeable man, showed us the list of Hendy's assistants and we got the name that way. In a few minutes Mr

Martin-James arrived. Marion put the picture in his hands and he immediately said: "It is by Desiderio." We thanked him profusely and withdrew.'

I find the following curious entry. 'At 6 p.m. I went to Frederica Rose's and found there Mr Bahr, the old China hand. Now 70 years of age, a fountain of anecdote, he does not stop talking. He said: "As everyone has heard, the Empress Dowager gave Kitchener permission to choose one peach-bloom vase from the palace collection. (At that time K'ang Hsi peach-blooms were the rarest and most admired Ch'ing dynasty pieces.) On the eunuch in charge opening the cupboard where such vases were kept, Kitchener, a ruthless collector of Chinese porcelain, had the hardihood to declare that the Imperial permission entitled him to take a pair, since peach-blooms were always in pairs, and so a pair was one piece. The eunuch swallowed this and handed over a pair." '

So far, said Mr. Bahr, the story was well known, but he could take it further. Kitchener, he alleged, tempted beyond control by the sight of more peach-blooms in the cupboard, proceeded to push his already fallacious claim another step. The word 'pair', as agreed in the present connection, did not mean two but only one object. He had received, in fact, one peach-bloom. But as peach-blooms always went in pairs, he was entitled under the august permission, to the pair of his pair. The eunuch, who had had his tip, allowed that this was a reasonable deduction. Kitchener went off with four peach-blooms. Later he sold two of them in New York for 40,000 dollars. Mr. Bahr assured us that he learned of this transaction from Kitchener himself, who asked him to have stands made to fit the pieces, not so easy, as peach-blooms have pointed bases like Roman wine jars. Next day Kitchener left Peking and was seen off on the platform by a group of senior officers and Chinese officials. So anxious was he about the stands that, catching sight of Bahr, who stood on the platform farther back, he beckoned him to come up and ignoring the notabilities gave him further instructions.

This was but one of Mr. Bahr's anecdotes. Another was that he had seen the Imperial Tablet, always kept concealed from view, which proved that the Emperor Ch'ien Lung did not belong to the ruling Manchu house, but was Chinese by birth. He also spoke of tea, the Imperial variety, vastly more choice than the tea which the Chinese Ambassador had told me about. Each leaf was rolled and bound with a red silk thread. To make a cup of tea one leaf only was required. By the end of the party Mr. Bahr and I were on friendly terms. He confided that his ambition was to write his reminiscences of the Court of China. As far as I know he failed to achieve this. He was a wonderful raconteur but no writer.

One of the people I met in the Princess Zeid's house was the Princess of Berar, whose father was the son of Abdul Hamid, the last Sultan of Turkey. She had married the Prince of Berar, the heir of the Nizam of Hyderabad, reputed the richest of the Indian princes. When I met her she was residing in Palace Green opposite the Iraq embassy. I first called on her in March 1952. A handsome woman of about forty, she had the most perfect command of English. Her appearance was cosmopolitan. I asked her how she had acquired such a mastery of the English language. She said she had had a wonderful English governess in Istanbul, who had remained her friend afterwards. Some time later she invited me to a party she was giving. 'The Princess was in an evening gown,' I record. 'Tall, pale and fair, with an aquiline nose, she had not the popular look of a Turkish princess. Hardly had I arrived when Somerset Maugham came in, froglike, inhuman, yet civil enough. There followed a stream of diplomatic notabilities. Frank Roberts said: "We have not met for some time, but I read you." He is one of my brother's friends.'

The Burmese embassy liked to keep in touch with me, for which cordiality I was grateful, since I remained deeply interested in what was happening in Burma. In January 1952 U Ka Si, the Burmese ambassador, asked me to have tea with him for a chat. Till the founding of the republic in 1948 he had been a member of the Indian Civil Service. I was taken upstairs to his room by Maung Maung Ji, the press attaché, a man I had known since 1930 when he gave evidence before me in the Sen Gupta case which made such a stir, as is described in my *Trials in Burma*. The Ambassador and I seated ourselves on a sofa and Maung Maung Ji saw to tea. I wanted to hear the Ambassador's view of how it was that the Burmese preferred to leave the Commonwealth in 1948. He said we had brought this on ourselves. Had we during the period of our rule in Burma from 1885 to 1942 (the date of the Japanese invasion) handled the Burmese better, studied their interests, as if trustees instead of rulers, they would never have asked us to go. Given the option in 1947 to stay in the Commonwealth or leave it, Burmese public opinion was for the latter course. There was still a substantial anglophil section in the country, but it was useless to think that at this stage Burma might follow India and, while remaining a republic, enter the Commonwealth. They were set on building their own future, he said. There were great administrative difficulties, but they must be overcome. He was referring to the disorder which prevailed in many parts of the country and which the government, under the Prime Minister U Nu, was striving to suppress.

U Nu had been over in England in 1950, when he gave a party at the Ritz on 18th February, to which I was invited. It was the first time the Burmese Embassy had given a London party. In my note on the occasion I have: 'Among those present were the Burmese Ambassador, U Ohn, a very young man with bright eyes and a soft manner; Rose Macaulay looking very old but wonderfully collected and alive; and Sir Gerald Kelly, the President of the Royal Academy,' whom I was very glad to see, having written warmly about him that very week in *Time & Tide* because he had saved Stanley Spencer from Munnings when the latter sought to have him prosecuted for obscenity. It was astonishing enough to meet him and Rose Macaulay at a dinner party given by U Nu, whose knowledge of English personalities was very small, and stranger still was it to find myself seated next to Henry Sherek, who at the moment was producing T. S. Eliot's *The Cocktail Party*. He had shown interest in my *The Motherly and Auspicious*, but nothing had come of it. Now, however, he assured me that the actress Anne Todd had asked him for a good part and that he was about to suggest the title role in my play. 'If she accepts,' I wrote in my diary, 'that would be a splendid stroke of luck after so many disappointments.' The diary goes on: 'When dinner was over I went, at U Nu's request, to sit beside him at the head of the table. We had never met before. I found him a plain honest man. He spoke of his hopes, the nature of his policy, his difficulties and finally of two books he had written, for which he wanted a translator and publisher. So absorbed was he in this tête-à-tête that he did not notice the time. He was still talking to me at the end of an hour, and had left his guests, of whom there were eighteen, to entertain themselves. I now noticed they were getting restive, as if anxious to go home but hesitant to rise from table before their host. On my hinting this to him, he called down in Burmese to the Ambassador at the foot of the table and ordered him abruptly to thank everyone for coming. This done, he stood up and declared in a disarmingly frank manner that he had over-looked the time, so wrapped up had he been in talking of his books. I found it a little embarrassing, for it was 10.30 by then. Moreover, as U Nu is not only a teetotaller, but will not offer drinks, and only fruit juice had been served, it was no wonder that conversation had flagged. But he was so ingenuous that his apology was readily accepted. It was interesting, too, to see what an earnest and rather naive personality was governing Burma in place of us.'

About the same date I had met Mr. Bowker, who had recently returned from Burma where he had been our ambassador. When I asked him what he thought of the state of things there, he quoted the old *mot*: 'They say in France, c'est grave mais ce n'est pas une désastre. In Burma it's the other way round. C'est une désastre, mais ce n'est pas grave. Nothing is taken very seriously in Burma.' There was some truth in this. U Nu wanted the population to take a serious view and thought that if he could revive the influence of the Buddhist church disorders would die down and the contend-ing factions unite for the good of the country. He was building an enormous pagoda near Rangoon and planned to make Buddhism the state religion. But as will be mentioned farther down his policy failed and he went out of power.

Other news reached me from friends in Burma. Noel Whiting, who had been so good to me when I visited the Shan States in 1938, still lived there. It was clear from what he told me that the government could not enforce law and order outside the towns and that travelling by train even on the main line from Mandalay to Rangoon was unsafe. He was so fond of Burma, however, that he was sticking it out and hoping U Nu would prove successful. That indomitable woman, Mrs. Erskine Childers, was also sticking it out, though no one quite understood why she did not return to her own country. She did not speak Burmese and had never sympathized with Burmese aspirations. To the last she remained an Irish lady old style, grand and rather stiff, though kind. She was a character.

Another source of Burma news I had at this time was Sao Van Tip (Lady Magic Mirror) who in 1938 when I visited the Shan States was the wife of the Sawbwa of Hsenwi (Million Umbrellas). A full description of her court at Hsenwi appears in my *Lords of the Sunset*. She now arrived in London and asked me to call. I had not seen her since 1938. My diary contains the following details. 'I found her at No 6 Earls Court Square. When I rang her bell she came to the door, looking just the same as she did in her own palace in Hsenwi fourteen years before. She brought me upstairs, where I met some of her relatives of the house of Kengtung, also on visit to England. She then dispensed tea. She had that inimitable air of manners and humanity which is typical of the Shan grandees. The conversation turned on how the Shan nobility had fared during the Japanese invasion of 1942. Most of the ruling Princes had hid in the jungle at first but the Japanese later induced them to resume the administration of their states under Japanese supervision. The Princess Thiri-Sandana[1] of Mong Pawn was unfortunate; she died of consumption in a jungle village. I invited Sao Van Tip to pay us a visit at Maidenhead.'

She drove down on 14th June 1952. To amuse her and her two companions, members of the Kengtung nobility, we took them over to Windsor Castle. The Queen was in residence and there was a big crowd of sightseers. We showed them round and were lucky to catch a fleeting glimpse of the Queen and the Duke of Edinburgh walking in the distance from one door to another. This pleased them very much. The sight of old Burmese cannon

[1] See her photograph gardening in my *Lords of the Sunset* and my description of her charming personality.

taken in 1885 from Mandalay and now on the castle battlements astonished them. On the way home we took them into Eton chapel. Back in Maidenhead they had tea. Sao Van Tip continued to delight me by her ease of manner and her superlative aplomb.

In September I called to bid her goodbye on the eve of her return to Burma. During the summer she had taken a trip to Paris and Switzerland, which she told me had been a great experience. I asked her what she felt about returning to the remoteness of Kengtung, where her house now was, for she had parted with her husband, the Sawbwa of Hsenwi. She replied that she had seen enough of the western world to satisfy her for the time being. To supplement her income she now dealt in precious stones with the Siamese, and had done so well that she had been able to afford her European tour. She said that she thought that U Nu intended to supersede the ruling princes and place the Shan States under one government of a non-royal type. In this she was correct. The great days of the Shan princes were closing. As I said goodbye I noticed the book she had been reading, one of Galsworthy's. I never saw her again; she continues to live in remote Kengtung and sometimes sends me a Christmas card or a letter.

Maurice Collis writing

12

Friendship with Bill Astor established

IT WAS DURING the war that I first got to know Bill Astor, then
heir to the Viscounty, to which he was to succeed in 1952. My
books made him want to meet me. His parents' house, Cliveden,
was about ten minutes' drive from mine, and he used to invite me
there from time to time. On 8th August 1945, the day the Ameri-
cans dropped the first atom bomb, I was asked to dine. At table I
asked his mother, the celebrated Nancy Astor, whether she had
heard about the bomb. Nobody present had listened to the
B.B.C.'s six o'clock broadcast. There was dead silence when I
repeated the news. Lady Astor didn't believe me, but Lord Astor
told the butler to bring the wireless into the dining-room. We
were at the pudding course when the news came through.

That year Bill Astor married Sally Norton, Lord Grantley's
daughter. They called in December and gave me a present of a
handsome volume from the Golden Cockerel Press on Voyages in
the South Seas. He had been a Member of Parliament for the
previous ten years and the circle of his acquaintance was wide. His
town house was in Upper Grosvenor Street and soon after his
marriage he bought Bletchington Park, a mansion and estate
close to the Duke of Marlborough's at Blenheim.

My friendship with him slowly ripened. In October 1950 he
asked me to stay a weekend at Bletchington. On the Sunday the
Duke of Marlborough asked us over for croquet at Blenheim.
Sally took me, as Bill declared nothing would induce him to play
croquet. We were shown into the Duke's study while a footman
went to fetch him. My diary has: 'In a few moments he came in,
tall, reckless looking with the Churchill face. He was in good

I

spirits as he liked Sally Astor. She kissed him and he shook hands with me pleasantly. When he knew I would rather explore the palace than play croquet, he took us round himself. It was to his hunting trophies that he first drew my attention. There was a wild buffalo head he liked in particular. But presently finding my eyes were resting on the objects of art, paintings, furniture and porcelain of which the various salons and corridors were full, he pointed out his favourites, such as a Roman bust from Herculaneum, at which Sally's spaniel barked, taking it to be a real and frightening person. Such busts are often very modern looking. The Domitian in the British Museum is the image of Mr Reid, Lowry's patron. So we walked on, past the battle tapestries of the Duke's great ancestor, to the 10th century Persian ceramics. I stopped to admire them, which was just right, for they happened to be an addition he personally had made to the ancestral collection. "I bought them myself," said he, pleased. "I didn't pay much. About a couple of hundred." We saw the dining table, laid ready, the Grand Hall, his own portrait (not a good one), the statue of Queen Anne and finally came to the huge polar bear rugs, at which the spaniel barked again. At the visitors' bookstall by the main entrance he gave me the palace guide book, an attractive publication fully illustrated. "It costs half a crown," he said, "but you can have it." The man in charge of the bookstall objected. "His Grace is always doing this," he complained.

'The tour of the palace over, the Duke went back with us to his study. He seemed exhausted and we prepared to leave. "Come again," he said to me, "bring your friends," and he saw us off to the head of the stairs, which we descended to a side door into the courtyard. The spaniel sat down on the mat and was dirty.'

During 1951 I continued to see Bill Astor. At this time his age was forty-four, while mine was sixty-two. He was not very robust, though able to go hunting, to travel backwards and forwards to the States, and to take an active part in managing his racing stable. He was much on the move and I did not meet him often enough to realize how badly his marriage was turning out. In April I stayed another weekend at Bletchington. A son had been born and was in the house, but Sally was away in America. It was not, however, until the following year, June 1953, that he told me what had happened. By then he had succeeded to the title and moved his residence to Cliveden, the family's great mansion on the Thames. My diary has under Sunday, 28th June: 'I went to lunch at Cliveden and found Bill outside the hall door. I had just heard that one of his horses had won the Oaks and, congratulating him, said the victory perhaps betokened a change of fortune for the better. By this time I knew in a general way that he had parted from his wife. To my remark he replied that he hoped I had second sight. Among the house-party in the drawing room was Freya Stark, with whom I had corresponded but had never met. I was delighted to see her, as I held her to be one of the leading stylists of the day. The gong went and we passed into the dining room, whose panelling was from the Pompadour's lodge at Versailles. How it came on the market I do not know. Somehow or other the first Viscount had bought it. As a multi-millionaire one supposes he could get what he wanted. For instance, he had managed to secure for the garden the balustrade of the Villa Borghese in Rome by providing the owners with an exact copy.'

After lunch we went out to sit on the terrace. Bill drew me aside as he wished to tell me about the breakdown of his marriage. He said: 'Sally suddenly revealed one day that she had been in love for years with an Oxford undergraduate. It was a complete and shattering surprise. We had never had a quarrel. It seems that her feelings for the young man were only romantic. She wanted to marry him and asked for a divorce. There was nothing for it but to agree. They were married.' And he went on: 'Sally does not realize that she has dealt me a cruel blow. She writes to me as if nothing had happened, and even talks of coming down here to visit me! We had been happy, I thought, but nothing I said could get her to change her mind. She was determined to leave me.' The shock, he told me, had affected his heart and blood pressure. Indeed, at lunch I had noticed once or twice how strained he seemed. Talking to me by the great magnolia on the terrace eased him for the moment. Freya Stark came up and the subject was changed. He said: 'I want to photograph you both,' and went to fetch a camera he had, a novelty which instantaneously developed and printed the photo. The result made us all laugh. Freya Stark looked like a sturdy cook, I looked much the worse for wear, and Lady Anne Cook, Lord Leicester's daughter, who had joined in, a beautiful girl who had been one of the Queen's train-bearers at the Coronation, appeared middle-aged and very plain. The joke amused us all. For the moment Bill forgot his troubles. When he saw me off he said: 'Now that we live so close you must often come.'

At this time I was engaged in writing my book *Cortes and Montezuma*, published the following year. I noted in my diary on 5th July: 'I have never undertaken a bit of work which absorbed me more. As one continues to ponder the story, it becomes stranger and more difficult to understand.' Bill Astor had recently stayed in Mexico for a short while. I told him of my book and asked him to run through the typescript and advise. He modestly disclaimed the capacity to guide me, but promised to read the typescript.

On 14th July the Julian Huxleys gave a party for Freya Stark. They were about to start on a lecture tour in South East Asia and were reading *Siamese White*. The tour would take them first to Borobudur, Angkor, Bangkok and then on to India, all expenses paid. In a way I envied him, but I had been in the East long enough. I believed I could write my books better by working quietly at home.

Among the several interesting people I met during the summer and autumn of 1953 were Frances Cornford, the poetess, at Cambridge, and Nevill Coghill of Merton, with whom afterwards I had so much to do. I had talk too, with L. S. Lowry, down from Manchester for his exhibition at the Lefevre Gallery, Bruton Street. He had sold £3,000 worth, a long way the best he had ever done. His rather sudden elevation into a prominent position in British art had in no way changed him. I noted: 'He was as awkward and inarticulate as ever. I said: "You have now become a great man." In his startled manner he replied: "Do you think so?" Yet behind his distracted old face peeped out something of the power which had enabled him to get where he was.'

A week later I came upon Scottie Wilson at the Gimpels. He too had recently had a great success. Since the day I found him selling his pictures at the men's lavatory entrance in Sloane Square, he had made a name in Paris, Switzerland and America. My note is: 'I saw him reposing in a chair. He got up and shook hands. He was pleasantly drunk. I spoke of his successes, so great since I first wrote about him in *Time & Tide*. He was rather incoherent and gave me his blessing.'

The same day I ran into Henry Moore in Bond Street. 'He looked well but a little haggard. We stayed talking awhile. He said that though a man who had not been laid up in bed for thirty years, he had recently had an operation for stone. It happened out of the blue and made him realise how uncertain was the strongest man's health. I looked to see if his international fame had in any way altered the charming simplicity of his character. It did not seem that it had. We were standing not far from his four strange abstractions in the façade of the Time and Life building in Bond Street. "It was lucky," he said, "that they were put in position during the coronation and so were hardly noticed. That way I escaped attacks and a disagreeable notoriety. Not that it would have mattered. An artist is only happy working. Or at least," he corrected, "an artist is much at a loss when not working." And he bustled off to go on with his work.'

I found dipping casually into the London round an existence that added to the happiness that writing afforded me, and much appreciated the further chances that friendship with Bill Astor held out. In 1935 King Gustav of Sweden was spending a November weekend at Cliveden and I had a message asking me to dinner on the 7th. I had met him when he was Crown Prince at the Oriental Ceramic Society. He was a close friend of Eumorfopoulos, and himself had a large collection of Chinese antiquities. I thought it might interest him now if I brought with me a red bowl I had acquired in Rangoon in 1930, a piece from the Emperor Ch'ien Lung's tomb which had been looted in 1928. The bowl was of exceptional quality. When I showed it at a later date to Sir Percival David, London's greatest connoisseur of oriental ceramics, he declared it to be one of a set made for the Emperor K'ang Hsi's jubilee in 1715.

On parking my car by the Cliveden hall door I found the porch in darkness and could not find the bell. So I knocked. There was no reply. Could I have got the date wrong? Continuing to feel the wall I came on the bell at last, the old-fashioned sort you pull, and dragged it hard. Almost at once lights were switched on and the butler, Mr. Lee, opened the door. I told him my difficulty about getting in. He excused himself and added in an awed voice: 'Lord Reith is coming. It might have been him now. I'd have caught it if it had.' He took my coat and showed me into the grand salon. Bill Astor, who had recently been to Scotland and to New York, was looking much better than when I last met him. In my diary is: 'I felt very delighted to see him. I find myself having a genuine affection for him.'

A few minutes later Lord Hailey was announced. At that date he was eighty-two. His career in the Indian Civil Service had been fabulously successful. On retirement from an Indian governorship he had become a Privy Councillor and received the O.M. I noted: 'He looks the old autocrat and has a cold smile.' He had driven down from London and no doubt wanted a drink. Bill saw to that at once, and introduced me to him. He had been to Corpus Christi College, Oxford, as an undergraduate and was now an Honorary Fellow. That had been my college and we were exchanging a few remarks when Lord Reith came in, very tall, an old sword cut across the face, a wild eye—a public figure if ever there was one. I had never met him before and now understood Mr. Lee's trepidation. He was clearly not a man to keep waiting at a hall door. Next appeared the dowager Lady Astor, Bill's formidable mother, who had been invited for the weekend because she was an old friend of King Gustav's. As Sally was gone, it was an interregnum. Nancy fell naturally into the role she had occupied for so long, that of mistress of Cliveden. I had met her only occasionally in the eight years since the atom bomb dinner in 1945. In face she looked older (she was seventy-four) but her gestures were as vivid as ever and her tone of voice as rallying.

There was a pause in the chatter as King Gustav entered the room. Though now about seventy, his appearance was little changed from what it had been at the Ceramic Society fourteen years earlier. He was in England on a private visit and arrived to stay at Cliveden without even a valet.

Dinner was announced and I found myself beside Hailey. As we went in, we politely urged each other to go first, which prompted him to make an apposite Latin quotation—from Cicero if I remember—a thing the first Viscount with his taste for Roman antiquities would have relished.

At dinner I was put on Bill Astor's right and could talk to him. Nancy Astor sat at the foot between the King and Hailey. As usual she managed the conversation. Though she intended to treat Bill as the viscount in being, she could not forgo altogether her old habit of bullying him. But he seemed better able to hold his own. The King did not speak much but seemed happy. Her manner to him was a mixture of licence and respect, which he found an agreeable English trait. There was some banter between her and Hailey. 'You are drinking too much,' she declared. 'Being so long in India has demoralised you.' He seemed to like her badinage and replied: 'I see you suspect me of lining my pockets in India.' And speaking generally to the table said that out there an Indian judge who, having taken bribes from both sides, gave back the bribe to the man who had lost, was called an upright man. 'How did Stalin strike you?' was the next question the old lady put to him; he had been on a mission to Russia. 'I thought he looked exactly like a Scotsman,' was his reply, as he gave a side look at a guest nearby. 'I told him straight out his régime was no different from the Czars',' she said, referring to a visit of hers to Moscow. ' "You dispose of your opponents without trial." "Of course" he said.'

After dinner I asked the King if he would like to see my bowl from the imperial tomb. He found this an agreeable break in the drawing-room conversation. I fetched it from the hall and he examined it with care, as he had never seen a similar one. As there was no magnifying glass handy, he went to his room to get his own. On his return Nancy Astor told Bill that he should have got it. 'Not at all,' put in the King. 'It was good for me to have to go.' He seemed to find it a relief to dispense with ceremony. He re-examined the bowl and made his observations to which Nancy Astor had to pretend to listen. He followed this up by some talk about his own collection of Chinese antiquities, describing how he had gradually come to admire Chinese archaic bronzes. He made a feeling reference to Eumorfopoulos and inquired about Staite Murray. But afraid of being tedious he broke off.

Lord Reith now said in an undertone to Bill that he was tired and wanted to go home. Ought he to wait till the King made a move? Bill said he would ask his mother. 'Don't tell her I'm tired,' said Reith apprehensively. He had the reputation of being tireless. 'Better leave it. I'll wait.' Soon afterwards, however, Lady Astor rose. King Gustav took the signal. The party was over.

13

Last and First in Burma

THE YEAR 1954 began by my wondering whether I could widen and vary my life by pursuing such literary by-ways as television, broadcasting, little film plays and some form of editorship. Though my association, as I have described it, with Korda had brought me in money it had led nowhere. I was not so foolish, however, as to neglect my writing, having recently published *Into Hidden Burma*, an autobiographical work taking the story of my experiences up to 1934, the year when this present book starts. I had also by the beginning of 1954 finished my excursion into Mexican history, *Cortès and Montezuma*, which was due for publication in October. The by-ways I mention would be a change from the steady and solitary struggle required for books. Television, for instance, would enlarge my audience, art editorship establish me further in the field I so much enjoyed. These were mistaken ideas. To cash in on my literary reputation in such ways would not enhance my position. But I was drawn to make a try. The line that Liàm O'Flaherty, for instance, had taken had an attractive look. I met him in my friend's, Elsa Barker-Mill's, house in March 1954. I used to read his books in the thirties when his reputation as an Irish novelist was high; his novel, *The Informer*, was much admired. I had never met him, till now in Elsa's house. In my diary I have: 'He was dressed in a white tweed coat and flannel trousers. His complexion was florid. He had a very easy man-of-the-world style of talk, and less the appearance of a man of letters than of an American film director. He told me that on the strength of his literary reputation he had been able to get onto the American magazine market and was now paid £1000 for a short story. In such happy circumstances why fatigue oneself by writing novels? he said. Make a literary reputation and then sell it, was his view.' Without going as far as O'Flaherty, it was tempting to think there were easy ways of increasing one's income by working, say, for the B.B.C. As distinguished a man of letters as Louis MacNeice was writing plays for it.

While in this lazy and stupid frame of mind I was in fact approached by one of the departments of the B.B.C. to write a series of film plays with Old Testament subjects and suitable for the children's programme. Tempted to try my hand I wrote one called 'The Burning Bush', which was produced on television. It was interesting to sit in a television operations room watching the huge machines, like antediluvian monsters, moving their snouts and prowling back and forth, and afterwards view the result on the screen, but it amounted to nothing. The remuneration was small and the work too impersonal. It was bound to damage one in the long run.

Another deviation from my proper sphere was suggested at this time. On 19th March 1954 Feliks Topolski rang up to tell me that a friend of his, an American called Singer, 'was starting an organisation to bring East and West together through the arts, and asked me to join them'. It seemed interesting and I agreed to meet Mr. Singer. Meanwhile I received by post a prospectus of what he termed his 'East West Art Centers'. My diary records: 'At 6 p.m. on 23 March I went to Feliks' house where Mr Singer was waiting. He is a young man of about thirty-six. It appears that while in India recently he was approached by certain backers who declared they had the funds to float an east–west organisation with an office in London and a quarterly journal to embody an East–West programme of lectures, exhibitions, etcetera. Would I accept the editorship of the journal? I enquired what was his financial backing. Would the editor's salary be adequate? Mr Singer assured me there was no reason for anxiety on that score. The backers were among the richest men in India. Ample funds would be forthcoming. He hinted—though here he was a little vague—that the organisation was not a purely business proposition. Behind the scenes were Sadhus or Swamis, whose aim would be to present a synthesis of eastern and western philosophic thought. This seemed too mysterious to swallow without further information. Mr Singer declared that he could say no more at the moment, indeed that he knew no more, but if he could count on my help and the co-operation of such distinguished people as I might persuade to lend their names, he would communicate with his principals, when more details would become available.' It did not strike me at once that the whole thing was but a version of what today is termed a 'group', inspired by the predication of some sort of eastern mystic.

After a talk with Singer a week later I was no wiser. The organization would come into existence six months hence; I was to edit the journal; I should begin by reading books of an un-specified kind. But I was not offered a retaining fee and was not told the names of the Indian backers. Instead of saying goodbye, politely but firmly, to Mr. Singer I told him I would like to see him regularly and be kept informed.

By the middle of July 1954, three months later, he had given me a few more facts. He related that he had lived in India for some months with certain mystic recluses and had attracted the atten-tion of an Indian millionaire called Birla, who had adopted him as his son. It was Birla who sent him to England to try and found the 'East–West Art Centers', a project which both of them had much at heart.

In August Mr. Singer assured me all was going well, though he admitted nothing had actually been done so far.

Towards the end of October, feeling that I really must get things a bit clearer I asked him to meet me in Topolski's studio. 'He made an effort on his side to be franker than I have known him,' I noted, 'and showed me letters from the Swamis. They were written in a mystic rigmarole, were of a general nature not directly touching the matter in hand.' Singer informed me that one of them, said to be wealthy, was shortly coming to Paris. The matter of finance would then be settled. 'One can only wonder,' I conclude. 'The project appears to be melting into thin air.'

The winter passed but nothing materialized. Topolski's attitude throughout had been optimistic. An East–West organization, of course, exactly suited him. He had been round the world, had done an infinity of drawings of notabilities and others in the places he had visited, particularly India and China, and had founded a publication called *Topolski's Chronicle* devoted to the reproduction of his drawings and containing on occasion notes of his own composition, the gist of which was not at variance with the supposed views of the Indians alleged to be behind Mr. Singer. Indeed, as his studio was to be the London headquarters of the movement, no wonder he hoped the plans would materialize.

On 17th February 1955 I went to his studio to meet Singer, though now very sceptical. I was told that in July there was to be an exhibition in Paris of Topolski's work, to be displayed in a Hindu atmosphere with swamis in attendance. I was shown some sketches of the sort of décor the swamis fancied. They were in bad taste. The art centres, their finance, the journal had nearly evaporated. One was left with a Topolski exhibition in Paris in rather doubtful surroundings. 'I still remain open to conviction', I noted, 'but am not very hopeful.' About a fortnight before the July exhibition was to take place I called to see Topolski. He had guests. The subject of Singer and the East–West Art Centers was not even mentioned.

This was the end as far as I was concerned of Mr. Singer and his swami backers. I did not see him again and told Topolski that I had informed the various persons to whom I had mentioned the art-centre plans, such as Lord Astor, Sir Steven Runciman, Lord Semphill, the Princess of Berar, that the project had fallen through. Mr. Singer continued, I was informed, to stay in London, in the hope apparently that his adopted father, Birla, and the committee of swamis would yet do something. When they did not, he withdrew to America and has not been heard of in London since.

While these silly negotiations were in progress, a new subject for a book had come my way, something far more in my line than editing an art journal backed by swamis. On 6th April 1954 the Burmese Ambassador gave a reception for the visiting Foreign Minister of his country. He was a man I had stayed with sixteen years before when in 1938 I visited the Shan States. At that time he was Sawbwa of Mongmit. I had written about him in my *Lords of the Sunset*. 'Ah, you remember that visit?' said he now, as if I could forget it. I was next introduced to Sir Reginald Dorman-Smith, who had been Governor of Burma in 1942 when the Japanese burst in and drove us out of the country. I had never met him before, though I was generally acquainted with his dramatic experiences. I found him engaging to talk to. Apparently he had been wanting to write an account of his governorship, the flight from Burma, the return at the end of the war, his relations with Mountbatten, the difficult passage with Aung San, the Burmese leader. 'But I can't write,' he said modestly. He had long wished to meet me and now hinted that he would like me to help him. Would I dine with him at White's after the party. I said I was dining with my publishers, but would write to him. 'Perhaps I shall see him again,' I noted.

As promised I wrote, and received an invitation to lunch at his house, Stodham Park, Liss, in Hampshire, a forty-mile drive from Maidenhead. I accepted and drove over. My diary for 17th April has: 'On arrival I found him having a gin with a Mr Battersby who had once been his A.D.C. The house is late Georgian with large grounds.'

He and his wife, Doreen, lived in elegant comfort, as she had a considerable fortune of her own. My diary continues: 'All day till 7 p.m. when I left he talked of his experiences as Governor of Burma and said he believed that only I could get on paper what was certainly a series of dramatic happenings.' As I listened to him I reflected how strange it was that I should be asked to write an account of the last days of our dominion in Burma. It had come round to that; an ex-Governor saw me as the person to do it.

Dorman-Smith believed himself to have been unfairly represented. I would know, he declared, how to put his case. He had been faced with issues of great complexity, and had done the best he could. He now made over to me his private papers. These, of course, required to be supplemented from other sources. There was much work ahead. I had so far written little where the testimony of living persons provided most of the material. A narrative of the sort is a delicate affair. If you consult people they expect you to adopt what they say, and tend to be offended if you do not. Some may become so keen to make your book a success that if you let them read the typescript they will labour to polish your style. In their loving care they may take you up over a comma. I remember a case where a lady put the matter in the hands of her solicitors because, in a photograph of a gathering out of doors, her deceased husband happened to be among those depicted, for which inclusion I had not sought her consent. In short, there are many pitfalls in such sort of composition. If you evade a charge of libel, you may yet arouse ill-will; if you escape an offensive letter in *The Times* correspondence page, many nasty things may be said behind your back. I am happy to say at once that in the case of *Last and First in Burma*, as my new book was to be entitled, I got away with only a few scratches. I attribute this partly to care, but principally to the amiable character of the persons concerned, and in particular to Reggie Dorman-Smith's unfailing good heart.

It happened that the first person I consulted was no friend of Mountbatten's, though I was unaware of the fact until I heard his trenchant remarks. This was Air Chief Marshal Joubert de la Ferté. Mountbatten, he said, saved Aung San, the Burmese leader, from being executed as a traitor, a mistake. Dorman-Smith was commended for being agreeable to the proposed execution. This was damaging for Dorman-Smith in ways which it would take too long to explain. I mention the fact simply to show what conflicting views were current. Everyone had his own interpretation of the alleged facts.

On 4th July I dined at Cliveden. Among the house party was Tony Keswick, a Director of the Bank of England, who had been in Burma just before the Japanese invasion as adviser to Duff Cooper, and stayed with Dorman-Smith. This was the occasion when Lady Diana insisted on taking off her shoes before entering the Shwedagon Pagoda, which so jolted the British community that she was called a pro-Burman, an unpleasant aspersion among them. It was alleged that Dorman-Smith, who, of course, had never done anything of the kind, admired her gesture but won-

dered whether she was right. At the dinner at Cliveden now he
would have been pleased to hear Bill Astor's remark: 'I think
Dorman-Smith should have got a peerage instead of the chilly
reception the India Office gave him on his return home.' Most of
the house party had hardly heard of him, but knew Lady Diana,
of course, and much enjoyed that part of the chatter.

I was now working hard on the book and had written some
fifty pages which Dorman-Smith was happy to commend. He
wanted me to meet a Mr. Ju, brother of U Saw, mentioned
farther back as the man hanged for the murder of Aung San, the
national hero. It was thought that Mr. Ju would have some
interesting things to tell me. I record: 'There was nothing secretive
about Mr Ju, when we met at the R.A.C., but he talked with so
little sequence that it was impossible to profit by what he said. He
kept on having double rums and became quite incoherent. However he promised to let me see certain documents. I can only hope
that they are relevant and that he will be sober enough to explain
them.'

Dorman-Smith, whom Mr. Ju called Sir Reggie, then took me
on to White's. A man came up who had once shot elephants in
Burma. This was thought good enough in the present connection
and he was asked to join us. After a while he rolled up his sleeve
and showed me how he had been tattooed with a magical diagram
by a Burmese *hmaw-saya* (sorceror), so as to render him invulnerable. I exclaimed: 'That is why you are alive and well today!'
'Quite certainly,' he replied. He was about fifty, had a powerful
jaw and roving eye. Dorman-Smith was pleased; he knew I had a
fancy for such oddities, and said: 'You see what White's can
manage for you!' It was certainly quite a feat for that famous
conservative club to produce a magical diagram conferring in-
vulnerability at four o'clock in the afternoon.

In this sort of haphazard way I collected information and
progressed pleasantly along the hard road of literary composition.
By October 1954 I had done more than half the book. That was
the month when my *Cortes and Montezuma* came out. Its reception
was good and it was soon translated into seven foreign languages.
The fly-leaf bore the dedication: 'To Viscount Astor, with warm

regards'. He gave a dinner party at Cliveden to mark the occasion. In the course of the evening he inquired about my Dorman-Smith book. 'You should meet Mountbatten,' he said. 'He will give you first-hand information about how he and Dorman-Smith hit it off. I'll introduce you. He is William's[1] godfather.' Mountbatten was Supreme Commander in Asia in 1945.

It was not until five months later that I met him. As designate First Sea Lord he had been away inspecting naval forces in the Mediterranean. By that time I had finished the book, which had taken me ten months to write. My diary for 31st March 1955 has: 'I received a letter inviting me to call at the Admiralty today, when Admiral Lord Mountbatten would like to have a talk with me. Accordingly at 4 p.m. I presented myself at the Nor' West door of the Admiralty, which is by Captain Cook's statue in the Mall by the Arch. A young staff-officer met me and I was taken to an ante-chamber, where I found Captain R. V. Brockman, Mountbatten's principal secretary, who had already done me some obliging turns. He announced that the Admiral was ready to receive me and ushered me in. Mountbatten got up from his desk with a smile of welcome. I told him shortly how the book stood and said it was in the matter of his and Dorman-Smith's attitude to Aung San that I particularly desired to hear what he would tell me. There followed an animated conversation lasting three-quarters of an hour. I thought him wonderfully young-looking for his age of fifty-five. He was in high spirits, throwing himself about in his chair, sometimes tilting his head right back, some-times leaning towards me, or perching himself on the little table I was sitting at.' His view was that Dorman-Smith had been too slow in his negotiations with Aung San. He did not realize quick enough that Aung San had the Burmese solidly behind him. Though hardly thirty he represented Burma. By the time his importance was accepted, he was committed to demanding a republic. He might have accepted Dominion status, argued Mountbatten, had Dorman-Smith put it to him earlier. I said: 'But Dorman-Smith was tied by his instructions from London, which did not go as far as immediate Dominion status.' 'As the

[1] Astor's son, the present Viscount.

Stanley Spencer painting *Christ preaching at Cookham Regatta,*
April 1962

man on the spot he could have put as wide an interpretation on his instructions as he thought the circumstances required,' was Mountbatten's response.

'Why, he would have been recalled if he had,' I said.

'Not if he turned out right,' said Mountbatten.

'A gamble,' said I.

'It's always a gamble!' said he.

I came away from the interview immensely pleased with Mountbatten's candour and warmth. 'I found him', I recorded next day in my diary, 'a person of exciting personality. The impression he gave was of courage and resolution.' There was little to alter in my text as it stood. By the addition of a touch here and there I made Mountbatten's view more clear. In the end Dorman-Smith and he were little divided in opinion. 'Till I read your book', Mountbatten said to me after its publication, 'I never properly understood how close in outlook we really were.' This was one of the biggest compliments I have ever received. It had been an exceedingly difficult matter to disentangle.

Dorman-Smith, settled at Liss, became a J.P. and High Sheriff of Hampshire, a quiet life compared with Aung San's, murdered by one of his own countrymen. It's all a gamble, as Mountbatten said. You never know where you are in this life.

14

Astor meets Stanley Spencer

By 1955, THE YEAR this narrative has reached, Stanley Spencer was painting large canvases of striking originality. I had kept in touch with him since the war years. It was tedious to have to listen to his talk, but it was never boring to see his pictures. He lived now permanently at Cookham in a hideous little house called Cliveden View on high ground half a mile beyond the main street. His first wife, Hilda, was dead; his second wife, Patricia, lived in a house called Moor Thatch, a pretty cottage on the edge of the village. His two daughters were with relatives. He much preferred living alone. I saw him to speak to at functions in London and Maidenhead, and when he called to see me or I called on him. On 8th February 1955 I noted in my diary: 'Went to see Stanley Spencer's latest at Tooth's Gallery in Bruton Street, a large canvas of men and women in punts, part of a huge composition on which he is engaged called *Christ preaching at Cookham Regatta*. I thought it one of his best, with its curious mood of flesh and emotion and his habitual great strength of composition and design. I found Daphne Charlton there, his great friend. She is a woman of over forty, plump and with a rather beautiful face, sweeter and more gentle than Spencer gives her in his well known portrait in the Tate. She told me of a great project of hers—to find a rich man who would provide Spencer with a hall in Cookham where he could hang his compositions, a permanent display comparable to his celebrated Burghclere chapel. Such a hall would have to be built and Spencer would have to be paid while he worked on the pictures. Though so celebrated, he was still very poor. I promised Daphne Charlton to do what I could.'

There was only one person I knew who might be willing to build such a hall, and that was my millionaire friend Bill Astor. Living so close, he might be inclined to act as patron.

Invited to dinner at Cliveden on Saturday, 8th January, I had found him mixing cocktails for his house party. I note: 'The butler came in and said dinner was ready. Astor reproved him: "The Duchess is not down yet." Soon afterwards the Dowager Duchess of Rutland entered, the mother of the present Duke. She had an air about her, but a very pleasant easy manner. I was deputed to sit next her at table. To open the conversation I spoke of her sister-in-law, Lady Diana, for whom I had such a liking.' I noticed that Bill Astor was more cheerful than he had been since the divorce from his wife, Sally, in 1953, though I did not know that he had fallen in love with Philippa Hunloke, whom he was shortly to marry. After dinner he showed me some paintings which he had recently added to his collection, a Renoir and a Dufy. So when Daphne Charlton a fortnight later mentioned Stanley Spencer's need of a patron, I saw a chance.

I did not meet Astor again until 9th April, as he was away in America. I went up to dinner. Mr. Washington, the butler, told me as I came in that I would be the only guest, except for Astor's half brother, Bobbie Shaw, who was staying in the house. Of this occasion I noted: 'I found Bill in the study, sitting by a wood fire. He seemed well but said he was not, that he had trouble with his blood pressure, an ominous sign at his age. He was taking, he said, some Indian drug, which had been used for centuries by old time Indian physicians. He complained of tiredness and said his doctor had advised him not to overdo things. The collapse of his marriage was a shock from which he is not completely recovered. But he appears less nervous than he was a year ago. His old mother is as tough as ever. She still, he says, plays eighteen holes of golf and does gymnastic exercises night and morning as well as taking a cold bath. She is about eighty. It so happened that in the course of the evening he said of his own accord that he would like to make Spencer's acquaintance, and get him to paint something for him. I said that could be easily arranged and dropped a hint about Spencer needing a patron, and he listened.'

Next day I drove over to Cookham and saw Spencer. The Wednesday following was fixed for me to bring Astor. 'The hall idea might very well appeal to him,' I said. 'Anyhow he'll commission you to paint something.'

On Wednesday, 13th April, I took Astor and Philippa Hunloke to Spencer's house. My note is: 'Spencer came to the door, his usual debonair talkative self. We went up the squalid stairs to the bedroom. The bed was covered with cardboard, drawings and photographs of paintings. There was not much of importance for Astor to see, as most of Spencer's paintings were at Tooth's. But there was Spencer himself, chatting at large about his doings, his father, the organist, his grandfather, the grocer, and mentioning that the suit he was wearing was a cast-off one the local doctor had given him. Though a celebrity he was still very poor. He had to pay for everything out of the £10 a week Tooth allowed him. Astor was amused and impressed by his personality and commissioned him to paint any picture he fancied at Cliveden. "I'll send my car to fetch you," he said.'

The result of the call was that Spencer secured the interest of a very rich man. Nothing, of course, was said about a hall, for Astor could not be rushed that way.

At this date, 1955, I had no notion of what was really in Spencer's mind in the matter. Not till 1960, when reading his papers, did I understand his extraordinary intentions. These are set out at length in chapters 18 and 19 of my Spencer biography published in 1962. His idea far transcended a Spencer gallery in Cookham containing a permanent collection of his work. What he imagined was a memorial to Hilda and three other women in the form of a sort of church-house with chapels dedicated to each and containing paintings of them, not portraits but scenes expressing a universal enlightenment through sexual union. I found later in his papers the fullest imaginable details of this plan, even the exact position of each painting being specified. The whole was to be summed up in an enormous canvas, seven feet by twenty feet, called 'The Apotheosis of Hilda'. The project was secret. He told no one. Daphne Charlton hardly understood more than that he sought a patron to finance a Spencer gallery in Cookham. That was all I knew, when I took Astor to see him. Had I known the whole explanation I could not have laid it before Astor. He would have had nothing to do with such a fancy. As it was, he went ahead like a reasonable man, kind and practical, bought Spencer's pictures, commissioned a portrait, made him an allowance, gave him a better house and, after his death, bought and arranged the present Spencer Gallery. He treated Spencer with great liberality. But he did not really know him, any more than did anybody else, for no one had read his intimate papers. His young friend, Francis Davies, had glimpses of what was beneath. He once said to me: 'On occasion as I looked at him the expression in his eye would be very wild, rapt and enigmatical.'

The day following Bill Astor's visit to Spencer he proposed to Philippa Hunloke and the marriage took place almost at once. They went on their honeymoon to the south of France and then to the Astor stud in Kildare. Soon after their return I was invited up to dinner. It was to be a big occasion for King Gustav of Sweden would again be staying the weekend. I arrived rather early. The Dowager Duchess of Rutland was the first guest this time to descend the staircase.

All the guests were members of the house party except myself. They assembled at their leisure in the big salon, where presently Bill Astor was mixing his well-known cocktail. His mother was staying, which made it rather frightening for Philippa, newly married, only about twenty-three and knowing few if any of the guests. 'It is her first big party,' Bill said in my ear. There was Lord Hailey, old enough to be her grandfather, as was King Gustav. Lord Bandon from Cork she had met, but not Lady Worsley, one of the Queen Mother's Ladies-in-Waiting, nor hardly the Dowager Duchess of Rutland. Another of the party was Sir Alexander Cadogan, O.M., aged seventy, recently retired after a distinguished career in the Foreign Service. It was a formidable array for a young girl. There was also Isaiah Berlin, Fellow of All Souls, a little dark laughing imp of a man, a noted wit, a brilliant talker, so dazzlingly clever as to be intimidating, but just right for a sparring match with old Nancy Astor, who, disapproving on principle of Philippa, assumed the mantle of hostess.

At table I was placed on the bride's left, King Gustav being on her right, with Nancy Astor on his right. I was able to talk to Philippa about the visit to Stanley Spencer and ask for her impressions. King Gustav presently joined in the conversation. My diary notes: 'He has the air of a savant, much dignity, a tone of authority suited to his rank, yet perfectly natural, kind and attentive. One of his expressions was to preface a remark with the phrase "for a man in my position". He declared that on his tours abroad he felt much freer than our royalty could feel because when he left Sweden a Regent took over with full powers and responsibility. Meanwhile Philippa was doing her best, keeping an eye on the butler and footmen, and joining in the conversation as required.'

When the ladies left the table Bill Astor came round and sat by me. I reminded him of his promise to get Spencer up to Cliveden and he said he would soon be seeing to that. When we rejoined the ladies in the salon, Nancy Astor took the lead away from her daughter-in-law in a ruthless manner. Taking her seat on a backless divan, she gathered a party about her, as she used to do when hostess at Cliveden. Lord Hailey, very old and somewhat fatigued, who had drifted aside with an illustrated paper intending to sit quietly and turn the pages, was hailed by her in a loud voice, 'Come on, old Hailey,' and when he pretended not to hear, she shouted again in her deep contralto, so that he had to put down his paper and join her group. He evidently did not like it much, but his experience of the world and acquaintance with her ways enabled him to capitulate with grace. She also secured King Gustav and started with Isaiah Berlin a rough and tumble political discussion, in which she played the managing female, the rôle which had made her famous. An hour passed when suddenly she jumped up, exclaiming at the time (it was 11.30), and led the women off to bed.

I took the opportunity to ask King Gustav if it was too late for me to show him a Chinese dish I had brought. 'It is never too late to look at a Chinese piece,' he replied. As we went into the hall where I had left it I told him how it had been fished out of the Bay of Bengal by a Japanese diver when I was in those parts. As a Sung celadon it must have been at the bottom of the sea for 700 years. When I handed it to him he remarked how weather-worn it was; the touch of the sea was on it. And the lines occurred to him, as he turned it this way and that:

> *Full fathom five thy father lies;*
> *Of his bones are coral made;*
> *Those are pearls that were his eyes.*

'Your dish has suffered a sea-change into something richer and stranger,' he said, pleased. I had also brought with me a copy of my *Cortés and Montezuma*, which was shortly to appear in a Swedish translation, their Book Society's choice. As the Swedes evidently liked it, and it was dedicated to his host, Bill Astor, I asked if I might present it to him. 'Of course,' he said, 'I would like to have it.' Bill had now joined us. 'It has reflections on the story which are quite fresh,' he said. The King got out his pen for me to autograph it, a gold-mounted fat pen, and I wrote quickly: 'Presented to His Majesty, the King of Sweden, by the author, Maurice Collis.' On his reading this it seemed to me the thought passed through his mind that he would have preferred me to write 'King Gustav of Sweden'. But he thanked me and put the book under his arm and went off to bed.

The reason I did not write 'King Gustav' is humiliating. I was not quite sure how to spell it.

15

U Nu in London

THE YEAR 1955 took its course. Final touches were given to *Last and First in Burma* as I talked over debatable points with those best qualified to advise me, such as Sir Gilbert Laithwaite, General Sir Thomas Hutton, General Kirby, the writer of the official history of the Burma campaign, and General Smyth, V.C., who commanded at the disaster of the Sittang bridge. When the book came out in February of the following year, Faber & Faber gave a big party at Claridges, to which most of those concerned were invited, a lively gathering of over a hundred. Everyone seemed satisfied. Reggie Dorman-Smith was immensely cheered up. His reputation, which had been so much damaged by malicious talk, was, he felt, repaired. He informed me he had been so worried that he had gone blind in one eye. The book, he declared, restored his sight. What most pleased him was that Mountbatten thought my interpretation a fair statement. He was further cheered by getting £1,000 damages in a libel action against Gollancz for publishing a book containing defamatory passages.

In point of fact he need not have been so despondent. There were people of standing on the Burmese side who were not ill disposed towards him. Before the book was out U Nu, the Burmese Premier, came on a state visit to England. He had been Premier since the death of Aung San in 1947. His tenure of that office was almost as long as Nehru's premiership in India. His former visit in 1949, when he gave the Ritz dinner party, was a private one. Now the guest of the British government, the Burmese Embassy arranged a reception for him at the Savoy on 21st June 1955. When I got there I saw many well-known figures from the Lords and the Commons, among whom U Nu was moving. Dorman-Smith had been invited, an amiable gesture on the part of the Burmese Ambassador which showed that in Burmese circles there was no reason to think that he would be other than welcome. When U Nu caught sight of him he went over for a chat. They sat down at a little table. U Nu invited me to join them. His book, about which, as related, he had asked advice at the Ritz dinner of 1949, had appeared in an English translation as *Burma under the Japanese*. I made a polite allusion to it. There was a chapter devoted to his detention in Mandalay jail under orders of Dorman-Smith's government, an amusing chapter in which he described how he was able to bribe the head jailer to release him at the very moment when Dorman-Smith, retreating before the invading Japanese, was halting at Mandalay on his way out. It seems that Dorman-Smith actually passed him on the road, without any notion who he was and, of course, the faintest idea that their next meeting would be at the Savoy in London in the present very altered circumstances. As we sat at the table he asked U Nu a question which showed how much he wanted reassurance. Had the Burmese not found the plans he had drawn up in Simla between 1942 and 1945 very useful? He had toiled to produce a blue-print for their prosperity. The British government had embodied his plans in a White Paper. Yet the Burmese would have nothing to do with him and his prosperity. Some months back I had been told by his A.D.C. Battersby when he visited me at Maidenhead that Dorman-Smith could not understand what had happened. Why had the Burmese turned down a man who was devoted to them and had worked years on plans to set them up again after the catastrophe of the Japanese invasion? He had been brooding on this ever since, Battersby told me. It seemed now that he was still miserable about it and that was why he put the question he did to U Nu at the reception.

At the moment the question was asked a press man took a photo of us at the table. I have it with me. It shows Dorman-Smith's agitated expression, my surprise and U Nu's calm. My diary runs:

'He replied evenly and kindly that he believed Dorman-Smith's plans had been of some use.'

The conversation was then changed. I mentioned my forth-coming book. It was agreed that I might publish U Nu's photo and that if I sent him proofs of the passages which concerned him, he would look over them and write. (In the event he expressed complete satisfaction with what I had written about him.) I noted: 'I found him very gentle and earnest. His expression was most charming. He was open, natural, mild, sympathetic, warm, eager to oblige. But as we spoke I saw other people waiting to catch his eye.' Lord Reading, then Minister of State, was standing by patiently, with someone he wanted to introduce. I whispered: 'The Marquess is anxious to have a word with you,' and got up. It was rather like the end of my talk with him at the Ritz dinner. He realized with a start that he had been neglecting the rest of the company. My diary winds up the scene thus: 'When it was time for U Nu to leave the reception he went away through the crowd which seemed to look at him with respectful warmth. The guests nearby seemed instinctively to line up and bow him out, some seeking a last word, some pressing his hand. It was a spontaneous display of feeling, a testimony to the general regard in which he was held and a wonderful solace for a man who thirteen years before had been locked up for demanding his country's freedom.'

But there is a verse that gives pause in the Buddhist sacred books: 'All suffering creatures who wander in the Three Worlds must needs endure the Eight World Predicaments.' And goes on: 'Not even King Mandhata, Lord of the Three Worlds, was free from rise and fall, separation and the breach of death.' U Nu fell not very long after his visit to London. On 20th July 1956 I met the man who was destined to take his place, General Ne Win, his Chief of Staff, for whom the Burmese Embassy was giving a reception that day. My diary records: 'I found him to be a pleasant, keen-looking youngish man. His wife was remarkably cosmopolitan for a Burmese woman, a good conversationalist, tactful and with a natural flair.' Next month I lunched with her and an American woman friend at a Chinese restaurant. My first impression of her charm and ease was confirmed. Of her companion I note: 'She asked, as an aperitif before lunch, for brandy mixed with port.'

When it became clear a year or so later that U Nu could not restore order and unite the warring elements in the Burmese state, General Ne Win set up the revolutionary government which he now heads and U Nu was detained at Mingaladon beside the golf-links, where before 1947 the whites used to relax. There for some five or six years he remained. He was let out only the other day, an even more fervent Buddhist than when he went in.

16

An excursion into English history

WHILE THE KIND attentions of my Burmese friends had kept me in touch with Burma to my great advantage and happiness, I chanced at this period, the middle fifties, to be tempted to write *The Hurling Time*, a piece of medieval English history which had no connection with the eastern subjects that hitherto had inspired me. I knew quite well it was an impertinence on my part to trespass into a region which had been thoroughly worked over by specialists. The reign of Edward III, his wars in France, the revolt of the peasantry, were an academic reserve. But I had become so captivated by a glimpse of the material, that I could not restrain myself. So to my intense enjoyment I wrote the book, depending upon what literary skill I had acquired over twenty years to carry me safely through. I had the prudence, however, to take some precautions. Charles Monteith, a Fellow of All Souls and one of Faber & Faber's directors, urged me to consult specialist opinion at Oxford and wrote on my behalf to a medieval historian there. On Sunday, 26th August 1956 I drove up to Oxford after lunch to see him. My diary runs: 'I had made a list of twenty-nine questions. It was perhaps expecting rather much that he would be able to answer such questions off hand. Some he just plainly said he could not answer, others he pondered, some appeared to agitate him, but what he did manage was to refer me to out of the way books and obscure articles in learned journals. I continued to question him for two hours and a half. By that time, though there were some left on the list, it was evident that he had had enough and, very grateful to him for his good offices, I took my departure. The visit reassured me. I felt that if I were careful and took my time the book ought not to seem too naive to the rather closed circle of the academic world. I am, of course, chiefly amusing myself by an excursion into a new subject, just as one enjoys a journey into a new country. So whatever happens I shall at least have had a happy journey.'

In the following June 1957, when the book was finished, I asked Sir Steven Runciman who was sitting next me at a lunch, with Charles Monteith only a few places away, whether I might dedicate it to him. He had just published the third of his famous volumes on the Crusades. His high reputation as scholar and writer (such a rare combination) was fully established. I was encouraged to make the request by the amiable notice he had taken of my books in general. He was pleased at my request and professed to be flattered. But such a show of good manners is what one has learnt to expect from Steven Runciman. After the publication I met him one day at Agnews. He reported to me that he had heard nothing but good of the book except in certain circles in Cambridge where some dons had asked what business had I to write such a book, a remark which he knew I would find entertaining. They were right, of course; there was little business in it. I only made £410 out of it, though I suppose the Income Tax people allowed me to set against the profit the cost of a French tour to inspect the battlefields of Crécy and Poitiers and the vale of Roncesvalles, a most thrilling experience. How one admires a government that gives an author grace without asking whether he enjoyed what he had to do! There was not a word of disparagement in the press. Altogether the book was a delightful diversion. But it was the last of its kind. I could not afford another. Fortunately, more lucrative openings turned up. I owed this good luck largely to the opportunities which my friend, Bill Astor, placed in my reach.

17

Nancy Astor in old age

I CONTINUED TO SEE Astor frequently when he was in residence at Cliveden. On 18th June 1956 I have: 'Dined with Bill tonight, along with Mrs Dewar, the widow of the whisky magnate, and an American cousin of his who had arrived that morning from the States. There was no one else. Mrs Dewar was a lively person.' Philippa was not present. I noted: 'Stanley Spencer has been painting Bill's portrait, which was on view. It is unflattering and makes him look worried. I said so and he said he was worried when Stanley painted it. He did not say why. After dinner we walked over to the swimming pool which Fiore de Enriquez, the sculptress, has adorned with a dolphin mounted on a bambino.'

This is the first mention in my diary of the swimming pool, afterwards to become world news.

I was up at Cliveden again on 30th June, to help at a tea party for visiting American teachers. Near the terrace I found Nancy Astor on a swing. She got off and, as she appeared not to know me, Bill mentioned my name. 'I know that gentleman,' she said severely. Later I came on her indoors. She began praising Bill. 'I consider him the most fitted of all my sons to head the family. He carries out faithfully his father's wishes.' In saying this her tone was very different from what she used when speaking to him. The diary continues: 'Her talk then suddenly shifted to herself. "Speaking as an old woman with not much longer to live, I can tell you something. We don't know where we are going." I said: "We have been all right here. Why shouldn't we be all right there?" At that she whisked away with an exclamation I could not catch.

Three American teachers were looking on and listening. Earnest women, they were deeply impressed.'

Some months later I called on Henry Channon to congratulate him on his knighthood in the New Year's honours list. 'I was ushered into the front salon by the butler, the room with the big portrait of his son. I had not seen Chips for two years or so. He shows little sign of advancing age except a tightening of the skin at his jaw. We sat down on a sofa under his array of old masters. "Have you seen Bill Astor lately?" he asked. On my replying that I saw him fairly often, he surprised me by saying that Philippa had just left him. This was startling news, as they had only been married a year. It is true, I had noticed a growing lack of cordiality between them. Chips said she had gone home to her mother the day before Astor returned from a visit to the States. Philippa was too young, as his first wife, Sally, had been, he added. She evidently disliked life in Cliveden when she saw it close up.'

This matrimonial crisis had evidently been working up when Stanley Spencer made Bill look so worried in the portrait.

Before I left Chips he began talking about Wavell, whose death had recently occurred. Who was going to write his biography? Lady Wavell had all the papers, which had been carefully arranged. Chips then suggested that I should. 'I will approach Lady Wavell,' he said; 'you will both come to lunch.'

Lady Wavell was, I think, already negotiating with John Connell, who in due course accepted the commission. I was perhaps well out of it. A full-dress biography of the Field Marshal would have been a most laborious undertaking. There were easier things coming my way.

On leaving Chips, who by a hardly perceptible movement had hinted that he was going out to dinner and must change, I went home and wrote to Bill Astor, who rang up next day to ask me to dine with him alone.

On getting there I found him in the library off the main salon. He was wearing his red velvet dinner jacket and plush slippers with his initials embroidered across the toes. He did not appear unduly upset. He mixed one of his very strong gin and brandy cocktails. Standing beside the blazing log fire he said: 'You have heard something of my domestic troubles.' I replied that I knew nothing till Chips told me two days before that Philippa had left him. He then came out with the whole story. In sum what he said was: 'After we had been married only four months, I began to find that Philippa was objecting to everything. This got worse, all was wrong, she found fault everywhere, wouldn't do this, was passive over that, never joined in happily. I did not know what to do. As time passed I grew more and more agitated. My blood pressure went up. It was like dealing with a person under a permanent resentment. The baby was born. Still no change. Finally, I could stand it no longer. I had to go on business to New York and I asked her to leave Cliveden before I got back. When I got home I found that she had left, which was a big shock, though I had asked her to go. I did not feel like Christmas here with a house party and decided to go to the aid of Hungarian refugees, who were trying to escape over the Danube. We used to sit up all night on the bank and help to ferry them across. There were long night hours with snow, but it did me good. I am now much relieved.'

So he said, yet he seemed still entangled in some sort of a psychological impasse. Was there a way out or not?

In the event nothing could be done. A divorce was eventually arranged.

I continued to be often invited to dinner at Cliveden. Nancy Astor was now generally there, able to sit at the foot of the table, as when the house was hers. On 4th May 1957 I had the place next to her. In her usual downright way she was expressing her views on the break up of the second marriage. Poor Bill! People had said such dreadful things about him. (In her own trenchant way, Nancy was a very loyal woman.) She made confidence after confidence. 'I told Bill I wanted to move back into Cliveden to support him, but he refused. I could have stayed in the wing with my own hall door. He wouldn't let me. He thought I'd interfere. What nonsense!'

Dinner was as luxurious as ever. We had jellied soup, prawns in white sauce, beefsteak with quantities of early vegetables and a cream pudding of particular excellence. As the pudding plates

Maurice Collis and his daughter contemplating the Stanley Spencer papers,
November 1961

were being cleared away she called down the table to Bill: 'I suppose a cheese course is coming.' The remark sent him nearly into hysterics. He declared he had carefully chosen all her favourite dishes, and waving his arms about he almost shouted that to be asked now for a cheese course was really beyond everything. 'There's no cheese,' he cried.

This ebullition did not disconcert her. She continued her conversation with me, reminiscences of her youth in Virginia and of the remarkable people she had entertained as hostess at Cliveden. I said to her that she ought to write her memoirs. She replied: 'Anyone who writes an autobiography ought to be put down!' At that she gave the signal to Bill that she and the ladies were about to leave the table. As they withdrew I said across the table to him that I had just been urging his mother to write her memoirs. In my diary is: 'He replied at once "You must write her biography." When the men were seated again he repeated that, if it could be arranged, he would so much like me to write a book round her and her numerous acquaintance, who included most people of note over fifty years. "There is no one else in the world", said he, "I would trust to do this." It all depended, of course, on whether his mother would fall in with the plan. In the drawing room afterwards the subject was not mentioned, but as I bade her goodnight she said she hoped I would lunch at her London house in Eaton Square.'

Thus, in May 1957, my book *Nancy Astor, An Informal Biography*, was first mooted. She was seventy-eight at the time. The publication took place two and a half years later. Bill did all he could to help but, as he reminded me more than once, his mother was very forgetful. The job was a delicate one. One day she would appear to be delighted with the project, on another would pretend she was being dragged into it against her inclination. Sometimes she would answer my questions with a resigned air, as if only because she knew Bill wanted her to co-operate. Sometimes she was so delighted with the memories which were called up, that she was at her most amusing and anecdotal. Or after inviting me to call at her house in Eaton Square she would ask me what I had come for; or invite people to meet me she thought might be useful, make me stay to lunch and introduce me to her relatives. And once she wired to Bill who was in Scotland, telling him to stop me writing the book. In it can be found a full account of how things went, I will not repeat myself here. Talks with her were never dull and I became gradually attached to her. She told me a quantity of droll stories, like G.B.S.'s last words and the tale called 'Let it rest', which I included in the biography. But after the book came out she pretended that she had never heard of me, nor seen the book, told her close relatives that the whole affair had been a grievous intrusion on her privacy, an allegation they seemed to believe for they reproached me; and when she met me at Cliveden or, on invitation, at her own house, would either look vaguely at me or pour a flood of fresh confidences into my ear. It was a wonderful experience, which I greatly enjoyed. The book, of course, is only a sketch, an outline, a collection of lively anecdotes, but Bill was satisfied, and that was all I cared about. Anyhow, it was all that could be done with the sort of material I had, a description of her as I saw her. I was not shown her correspondence nor the correspondence of those in closest touch with her. Her formal biography remains to be written. There are many interesting queries to be answered. Why did the Viscountess Astor, M.P., in her sixties, ride madly pillion over the country behind Lawrence of Arabia, by then half off his head? Was she a fanatical teetotaller because of the horror she felt long ago for the way her first husband drank? How would a psychiatrist explain the apparent love-contempt she had for her son Bill? How did she really stand with her husband, Waldorf? Her future biographer will, no doubt, solve those problems.

Writing the book suited me ever so much better than would have a biography of Wavell. It also yielded in royalties four times as much as my book *Last and First in Burma*, as it went well in the American market. It broadened my outlook, saved me from getting too much into a rut with Far Eastern themes and led to Bill affording me other opportunities. My connection with Cliveden was made closer. In short, it was another of my bits of luck.

18

The return of the potter, Staite Murray

IN THE EARLY PART of this book I mentioned Staite Murray, the potter, whom I got to know after my family and I went in 1937 to live in Maidenhead. He was then at the height of his fame as a potter. As great a connoisseur as Eumorfopoulos considered him the leading potter of the day. When he left Maidenhead for Rhodesia towards the end of 1938, his house was let and he locked up his studio in which were hundreds of his pots. I understood at the time that his intention was to return in twelve months or so. But overtaken by the war of 1939–45 he settled in Rhodesia and let the years pass without communicating his plans to his agents here or to me, who had been a close friend. His studio, a sort of large greenhouse, became gradually dilapidated and was invaded by creepers and every sort of weed. It was situated about a couple of miles from my house. Occasionally I peeped in and could see the pots, worth thousands of pounds, lying there unprotected for the glass was broken in places.

On 2nd July 1957, nineteen years after I had last seen him, I was astonished to hear his voice on the phone. He had returned, was at his studio and wanted to see me. The diary entry states: 'My daughter and I went round and found him in one of the rooms off the greenhouse studio. He is much aged, of course. When he left he was fifty-seven and now is seventy-six. It was extraordinary to reflect that at the height of his reputation as an artist he had thrown up everything and buried himself in a remote village in Africa. Had he done any potting there? No, he said, he had not touched a pot for nineteen years. He lived as a recluse, wrote poetry, studied

Buddhism and practised meditation in the Zen manner. What had brought him back to England? He felt that he must sell his property, ascertain whether his pots were safe and in the interest of his heirs arrange for them to be sold. Would I help him? I assured him I would do so and that I did not anticipate any difficulty, as he had not been forgotten. When it was known that some hundreds of his pots, made over twenty years ago, were coming on the market it would cause a sensation in the art world. A West End exhibition could be arranged. At the moment he is picnicking in the studio, cooking his own meals and sleeping on a sofa. The bathing facilities are those of a camp.'

On my next visit ten days later I found that he had washed his pots, some two hundred. One perceived that many of them were of the highest quality. In the meanwhile I had made inquiries in London and knew of two leading galleries eager to offer him an exhibition. Besides his pots he had certain works of art, including a Velvet Breughel, three early Ben Nicholsons, a bell of the Han dynasty and a splendid Oceanic sceptre. I was to arrange for the sale of them also.

During the ensuing weeks I managed to fix an exhibition at the Leicester Galleries for the spring of 1959. I also negotiated as best I could the sale of his pictures. I saw him frequently. He used to come to my house and liked looking at my collection of Chinese ceramics, pictures and other objects of art. 'He always', I noted, 'makes a good impression on other guests with his old smiling face. The way he rambles on about Buddhism does not seem to put people off.'

A member of the Thai nobility, Luang Sitsayamkan, whom I had met in 1933 on a boundary commission, as related in my book *Into Hidden Burma*, happened to be on a visit to England and called on me at Maidenhead with his wife. I thought it would interest Staite Murray to talk to some real Buddhists and took them round to see him. By that time he was not living in such squalor, for his nephews, shocked at the way their celebrated uncle was roughing it, brought a caravan for his use.

As we drew up in his garden I saw him walking from the studio to the caravan and pointed him out. His clothes were of the shabbiest and his general appearance dishevelled. 'Is that Mr. Staite Murray?' exclaimed Madame Sitsayamkan in surprise, finding it hard to believe that so famous an artist should look like a tramp. But his manner was very cordial and they soon took to him. He placed chairs for us outside the caravan. Determined to take advantage of a visit by Thai notabilities he began at once discoursing on Buddhism and asking Sitsayamkan questions. I noted: 'He was very confused and showed himself ill-informed, but Sitsayamkan was tactful and patient. I found it a bit tiring but they enjoyed the novelty of it and at the end signed his visitors' book at his request in both English and Thai. Some friends of his in the caravan came out to join us but he did not think them cultured enough and they were told to wait in the bushes.'

Of a later visit I have: 'Louise and I found him asleep in his caravan and while waiting for him to wake strolled in the garden. Then I saw a quantity of broken pots, ones he had smashed because dissatisfied with their glaze or form or for the reason I have given further back that he believed them to be tenanted by evil spirits. Some of the pieces were as large as half a jar and of excellent quality. I resolved to ask his permission to take a few of the best for my rockery. When he joined us I mentioned this and though not very happy to let me have bits from pots which had harboured devils, he said I could take what I fancied. I noticed nearby a stone head among nettles and when I admired it, he gave it to me,[1] saying he had bought it in Sicily in the twenties. To this he added an African carving of a tortoise in wood, which he gave to Louise.' He was naturally generous with presents and I suppose he felt grateful as we had run about a good deal on his behalf.

He next asked me to help him to select the best pots for the exhibition and to price them. If I did that, he would let me choose a pot for my collection. Pricing them was a long job. On 8th November I spent from 2.30 to 7.30 p.m. with him, sorting and debating prices. It was a cold job, too, for there was no heating in

[1] When washed it turned out to be marble, late Roman, a child's head with mouth wide open, evidently the conduit for water to a tank. Neither I nor Staite Murray knew it was Roman.

the huge studio beyond a small oil stove. In the end a reasonable price list was fixed. I bade him farewell that same November night as he was leaving for Rhodesia very shortly. He had managed to sell his pictures, except the Velvet Breughel, which he was taking back with him to Rhodesia and intended to give to the Buddhist Lodge which he had founded there, a handsome present though, one feels, not quite suitable for a Buddhist shrine.

I never saw him again for he died in Africa a few years later. His exhibition at the Leicester Galleries in 1959, which he did not attend, was a great success. He made over £3,000, an unheard of sum for a potter ten years ago.

19

London occasions

THERE WERE OTHER curiosities in the art world besides Staite Murray. Here I give a few brief glimpses from my diary of personalities I met at this time.

The first is the strange impression I had of T. S. Eliot at Fabers on 1st January 1957. While standing in the hall a moment on my way out: 'I saw him descending the stairs. He was dressed in dark clothes, an overcoat, a soft hat. His face was exceedingly lined and weary. He passed by and out through the hall door, drooping with gloom and as it were dazed with despair.' This was one of the few times that I came face to face with him, though he was one of Fabers' directors. On this fleeting occasion he made so curious, almost occult, an impression on me that I described it in the above words the moment I got home.

At one of the Princess Zeid's famous parties at the Iraq Embassy I was introduced by Terence Mullaly, the art critic of the *Daily Telegraph*, to Maria Carras, the wife of the Greek millionaire shipowner of that name. Following our first acquaintance she told me that she wished to entertain the Princess Zeid to a luncheon and asked me whether I could suggest the names of some artists or literary figures whom the Princess might like to meet. I gave her a list and invitations went out for 11th June 1957. Maria Carras's house was an attractive place. I had noticed when first I called on her a good Murillo, a large Harpignies, a Pissarro, a Degas and a Van Dyck of Negro Heads. There were Ming celadons, classical Greek terracottas, Cretan pots and Cycladic figurines, not an important collection like, say, Mrs. Seligman's, but wholly authentic and luxurious, just the place for a select luncheon party.

The guests on my list who had accepted included Mariquita Sedgwick, Bill Astor, Steven Runciman, Stanley Spencer, Julian Trevelyan, John Rothenstein of the Tate and Charles Monteith of Fabers. Arthur Waley had been tempted to come, which pleased me best of all, for my admiration for him as a writer and an orientalist was unbounded.

As the luncheon proceeded the guests, enlivened by the best wines and a fabulous cuisine, seemed to find the occasion to their liking. 'Stanley Spencer, though too talkative for my patience, was such a curiosity as well as so celebrated a painter, that he made a not disagreeable impression. Abominably dressed, crumpled and rather dirty, he was immensely animated and apparently Charles Monteith, who was next to him at table, accepted him as a character and in his amiable way pretended to gather what he was talking about. Arthur Waley made a powerful impact by the dreamy impassivity of his features. Of him the Princess Zeid exclaimed in my hearing that he looked the savant par excellence. When Bill Astor, struck by the plainness of Mariquita Sedgwick's clothes, enquired from Louise who she was, he learned that she was a rich woman who had befriended me on my arrival from the East in 1934, whose collection of Chinese ceramics, jades and so on was the choicest in London and worth half a million, that no other woman connoisseur had so high a standing, and that her clothes, though superficially plain, were, as any woman could see, the product of some very expensive dress shop. His Lordship gracefully corrected himself, saying that no aspersion on her costume was intended, for its very plainness bespoke her taste.' I have recorded a remark she made to me on a previous occasion about Arthur Waley: 'I am rather afraid of Arthur Waley. If you speak to him in a general way to make conversation, he will not answer. If you venture on some observation about China, he contradicts you and proves that you are childishly misinformed.' My reply was that I had been dressed down by him in a similar way, but that I thought he was good for us. One left him feeling freshened up and tightened up. My diary entry of 17th April 1956 has a view of him: 'I was walking through St James's when I came on Arthur

Waley and Beryl de Zoete sheltering on a doorstep of a restaurant from a passing shower. He hailed me: "Here comes Maurice Collis." He was wearing a battered beret and looked well and vigorous. His eye as usual was very keen. Beryl de Zoete nowadays is a shrunken little figure, bent and huddled, with a nervous tic in her face. After a little conversation on the step Waley suggested we should go into the restaurant and have an ice. Sitting at a table he spoke of a recent article of his on Captain Anson at Canton which was in the current issue of Peter Quennell's periodical *History Today*, a subject which interested me as one of the liveliest chapters in my *The Great Within* (published in 1943) was about Captain Anson in Canton just before and after he sank the great Acapulco treasure galleon. I was struck as always by Waley's incisive brilliance, his teasing humour, the vitality of his mind. So we conversed until he left with his old companion to look at a Japanese exhibition at the Arts Council in the square. On bidding him goodbye and telling him what a great pleasure I felt at meeting him, I noticed with surprise, for I had forgotten it, the abrupt cold manner in which he made his adieu, an unfortunate trick of his which must have offended or abashed many people, until they understood that it was no more than a mannerism and meant nothing personal to them.'

Well, here was this eminent personage at table with me again. He was my age, at the time sixty-eight. He has recently died. I remained to the last a devoted admirer of him as a great scholar and master of a soft delicious prose style, so different, as Bill Archer, head of the Indian part of the V. & A., once said to me from 'his intimidating manner in conversation'. He can fairly be classified as another curiosity of the day.

I wind up my diary note on Maria Carras's luncheon with the sentence: 'I have never seen Sir John Rothenstein make such an effort to be polite.'

Bill Astor, who had entertained me so often, seems to have enjoyed the lunch, for shortly afterwards I heard him tell his mother that I gave wonderful London lunch parties, to which the redoubtable Nancy replied she didn't believe it.

Maria Carras's son, Costa, was not at the lunch as he was at

Oxford attending to his studies. I was firmly of the opinion that he would get a double first. When he got a first in Classical Moderations, I was convinced the first in Greats would follow, for he was patently a classicist of mark. Sure enough he did get a first in Greats, thereby achieving the highest academic distinction, though anomalously it carries no letters to be quoted like D.Litt. after the name. The world will hardly learn that you are a Double First or, indeed, have even heard the expression. I immediately sent him a telegram of congratulation. The telegraph people, always eager to help by editing telegrams deemed obscure, took the words Double First to refer to twins and emended the text accordingly. What an anecdote this would have made to relate at the lunch! One can but compare it to Nancy Astor's telegram to her son, as edited in the post office. 'Please stop Maurice Collis from writing my wife.'

One more character of the period comes to mind—Augustus John. I have a glimpse of him in my diary for 11th March 1961 at a party given by Dudley Tooth when some of his pictures were on private view. 'There was an idea,' I wrote, 'that at 83 he would find it too tiring to stand and a chair in an alcove was provided for him. But he insisted on standing in the crowd. He looked very old and unkempt. There was a noble and rather disapproving look on his face, the sort of look that a great dog sometimes has, the disapproval being mellow and in some sort droll.'

20

The death of Stanley Spencer

STANLEY SPENCER BECAME widely famous in the nineteen fifties. He had been knighted and a university conferred a doctorate on him. But what did his paintings mean? Were they folk renderings of the biblical story? They were very queer for just that. And a lot of them had no direct bearing on holy writ. Were they in a sense religious? If so, in what sense? These questions were hardly raised, but some people would have liked more light on the problem. It was known to a few that he had written lengthy notes on what had inspired him to paint as he did. His monologues, as far as the listener could make out, appeared to be dissertations on this very point. It mattered little whether his auditors were paying attention. He was addressing himself and in this way formulating his ideas. It can be said that by 1958, the year before he died, his intimates, with very few exceptions, were ignorant of the contents of his papers and had formed no coherent idea of the beliefs which apparently lay behind his paintings and were the constant subject of his talk.

At this date I sometimes met him at Cliveden. Bill Astor had got to know him better while the portrait was being painted. Spencer was even occasionally asked to dinner. The first time this happened he remarked to his host how much he appreciated the honour. 'No one has ever asked me to dinner before,' he remarked in his candid manner. 'I have only been invited to functions.' He had, of course, no evening clothes, but managed to borrow a dinner jacket. He had the curious habit of wearing his pyjamas under his evening suit. The ends of his pyjama-trousers would protrude. He showed no trace of shyness no matter what the company and made no change whatever in his mode of conversation, which always centred on what he had written that day in the pads. When he dined at Cliveden, the same fashionable crowd would be there, racing people at Ascot week, dons in the vogue, members of the House of Lords, diplomatists, American notabilities, Generals, Admirals, famous military figures like Lord Alexander, Duchesses such as the Duchess of Rutland or Roxburghe, writers like Enid and Walter Starkie, Freya Stark, Peter Fleming, Snow, and wonderful figures of the great world like Nubar Gulbenkian. Among such a crowd, say some thirty at dinner, served with all the luxury of that house, food, drinks, silver, flowers in profusion, one would sometimes detect Stanley Spencer. I remember once sitting between him and the Earl of Derby when the ladies had risen. Lord Derby was talking about horses, but Spencer would manage, if the Earl paused, to take up his parable from the pads. The Earl was too polite to move to another part of the table, as he might have done at that stage of dinner. He could not tell on what Spencer, in his bright happy voice, was holding forth, but he put on an appearance of attention. I had intervened when I could to give him a chance to return to racing, but presently was called away by Bill who wanted me to come up and sit next him, as Prince Aly Khan, the Aga Khan's son, had expressed a wish to meet me. As I left my seat, I saw the Earl's face on which was a hunted look, for Spencer had opened up relentlessly from the point he had reached in his exposition. For me it was a happy moment. Aly Khan had the most perfect manners of any man I have ever met.

On 30th December 1958 when I was sitting alone with Bill Astor after a small private dinner, he told me that Spencer had been taken suddenly very ill and was to be operated upon. The diary has: 'It was said to be cancer of the stomach. Bill thought his chances small. He had been to see him in the Canadian Hospital (in the grounds of Cliveden) before dinner and had given him a book of Osbert Lancaster's cartoons to cheer him up. He told me that he had instructed the hospital to put down all expenses to him—a private room and everything else.' In point of fact Spencer refused the private room. He preferred the open ward, where he could talk at large. 'He also said that if Stanley recovered he had resolved to finance him to the extent of £1000 a year.'

The operation followed, a desperate attempt to cut the cancer out of his stomach. On 15th February 1959 he was well enough to dine at Cliveden. I noted: 'Among the guests, including the charming old Lady Gowrie and her grandson, the Earl of Gowrie, the Duchess of Roxburghe, and the Warden of St. Antony's, Mr Deakin, was Stanley Spencer, recovered from his operation. His colour was good and his appetite normal, but so gravely has he been cut about and threatened that one cannot say if he will long survive.' One glimpsed nevertheless his powerful character. He knew he was doomed, yet he was not yielding to fate, nor to principalities or powers, or anything else. He would go down painting and trying to explain the conception of life and death which lay at the root of his vast compositions and to which no one had the clue so far.

Bill Astor, feeling that Spencer could not safely continue to live by himself at Cliveden View, his house a mile beyond the village of Cookham, bought for him Fernlea, the house in the main street where originally the Spencer family had lived. He transferred himself there with all his papers, on the careful collection of which he anxiously insisted. As has been explained he had an enormous programme, the painting of a vast series of pictures to furnish the building, not yet built, which was to contain chapels to the four women he had loved and the vast 'Apotheosis of Hilda', which he had begun. Patched up as he was after the dreadful operation, he was not really strong enough to grapple with even one of the large canvases he had in view, but for all that he rigged up the half finished 'Christ preaching at Cookham Regatta' and piling a chair upon a table strove to reach the top section. One day his chair slipped and he fell off the table gravely hurting himself, but unbeaten renewed his labours.

I went to see him there on 3rd September to talk about the book which Bill Astor was pressing me to write before it was too late. Spencer told me he had contemplated such a book more than once in the past. Publishers and critics, such as Sir John Rothenstein, had made proposals, but nothing had come of them. The kind of book he had in mind would have long verbatim transcripts from the pads. Explanations here and there, editing and a general introduction would be done by a critic. My diary comment on this runs: 'This did not seem to me promising nor what Astor has in mind. Spencer's writings could only be presented with severe editing. It seems doubtful if he would submit to this.' I came away feeling a biography of him could not be written in the way he suggested. It could only be done by a professional writer. This was also the view of Dudley Tooth, the well-known art dealer, who was Spencer's chief trustee. 'Nothing can be done', he said to me, 'until after his death, when his papers can be examined by a suitable biographer.' Tooth knew that Astor wanted me to undertake the task and was in agreement with his lordship that the work might be entrusted to me as soon as the papers passed into the keeping of the trustees, who besides Tooth consisted of a Cookham solicitor, Mr. Shiel, and a wealthy brewer, Mr. Martineau. Fabers were informed of the situation, but being ignorant like everyone else of the sensational contents of the Spencer papers, they showed no eagerness to take up an option.

Meanwhile Spencer had a relapse and had to leave Fernlea and return to the Canadian Hospital. The cancer had recurred. His case was hopeless. No further operation was possible. The Vicar of Cookham, Mr. Westropp, and his wife, offered to look after him. He stayed with them for some weeks, when he again had to return to the hospital where he died on 15th December 1959.

His funeral took place on 18th December at Cookham. The description in my diary contains the following: 'Spencer's body was cremated yesterday and the little box containing his ashes was brought to Cookham for burial. I arrived for the service at 11.45 and had a word with Bill Astor who was standing at the church door in a top hat and morning coat. He told me Spencer was in full command of his faculties to the last. He had been in much discomfort but not in acute pain. The church was full. Among those present, besides Spencer's relatives, were Dudley Tooth, Terence Mullaly and the President of the Royal Academy. Astor gave an address standing on the steps of the choir, a personal tribute to his friendship with the dead genius and a lament that he had not lived to finish the many paintings which he had planned. (Spencer's plans were in fact far more ambitious than was understood until his papers were read and his scheme for a Temple of Love with its hundreds of paintings was revealed.) The service in the church over, we went into the churchyard for the burial of the ashes. Mr Westropp read the final passages of the office and after the words "earth to earth, ashes to ashes" placed the box in a little hole. It seemed no more than a memento of the person who had gone. The body had vanished into the air. When I heard Westropp reading the sentence "I heard a voice from heaven saying unto me, write", I was deeply affected. And when, after the concluding passage, I turned to Astor, praising his speech for its humanity and sweetness, I was overcome and had to move away to the wall of the churchyard with Louise, who helped me to regain my composure. Before leaving I had a word with Dudley Tooth and asked "What is now going to happen about the book on Stanley?" '

His reply was to assure me that, as he now had the legal right, he was sending at once for the papers, the hundreds of thousands of words Spencer had written about himself and his ideas, which no one had yet read.

This he did immediately. He despatched his chauffeur, and every scrap of paper in Fernlea was collected into three large packing cases, put into his Bentley and taken to his gallery in Bruton Street, W.1. He did not attempt to read any of the papers, which were in the utmost disorder. A glance at them told him the right course was to entrust them to a qualified biographer. Who that biographer was to be must now be decided. An agreement on this point by the three executors under Spencer's will, Mr. Tooth, Mr. Martineau and Mr. Shiel, had to be reached. Tooth reported the position to Astor.

On 20th January 1960 I attended the Spencer memorial service in St. James's Church, Piccadilly. I sat down by myself somewhat apart from the congregation. 'Presently someone came from behind and took his seat by me. It was Astor. The oration was delivered by Westropp, who spoke well and with feeling. The service ended with the Russian benediction, called the *Contakion for the Departed*, chanted very beautifully. As we left the church Astor whispered that he thought the arrangements for me to write the Spencer biography were progressing satisfactorily and asked me to dine at Cliveden on 31 January, when the Spencer executors, Shiel and Martineau, would be present. Tooth was abroad.'

The dinner of the 31st was one of those large Cliveden occasions. Shiel and Martineau were there, as was Spencer's brother, Gilbert Spencer, an Academician, but their business with me was presented as by the way. The principal guest was the American Admiral, Robert Dennison. I noted: 'He commands the great Atlantic fleet, the most powerful fleet in the world, a big thick-set man with an engaging manner though he looked the traditional sea-dog. I was much taken with him. At table the brewer, Martineau, a tall thin man with a Foreign Office look, sat opposite me. Other guests were Lord Grantley, Bill's former wife's brother, Wilfred Blunt, Mrs Cooper, formerly the Countess of Gowrie, and Bronwen Pugh, the dress model and daughter of the County Court judge of that name. The rumour that there exists an understanding between her and Bill may have substance. Her expression is charming. She told me that old Nancy Astor had spoken nicely to her. Perhaps there is an engagement here. A third marriage?' After dinner I was taken aside by Martineau. He said at once that he and Shiel were in favour of my being entrusted with the Spencer papers though the executors would have to decide what papers should be withheld from me as it was rumoured that some had indecent, some libellous passages. The matter of a publisher was already in train because, though Fabers had expressed no interest, Collins had thought a book a good idea and was ready to discuss a contract with me.

When Tooth returned from abroad, he sent me the papers. His Bentley arrived at my house on 11th March with the boxes, three large packing-cases. A first examination showed that the papers were not arranged in any order. Most were undated. They were written in pencil, sometimes on lavatory paper, sometimes in cheap notebooks, the pads. It was clear that it would take six months or more to sort them and get them into chronological order. I had no idea what I should find in them.

Maurice Collis in Glen Malure, Co. Wicklow, 1963

21

The Stanley Spencer papers
and what they revealed

WHEN THE PACKING-CASES were opened and the vast accu-
mulation of Stanley Spencer's discourses on his life and art, together with his letters to the four women, Hilda Carline,
Patricia Preece, Daphne Charlton and Charlotte Murray, were
revealed, the handwriting difficult to decipher on its thin
paper, often on both sides of a sheet, it was a spectacle to make
a biographer quail. Could I ever build sense out of what looked
such a muddle? Was it likely to be worth while? It would take
months. Fortunately my daughter, Louise, offered to help. An
experienced writer and scholar herself, and also acquainted over
the years with Stanley Spencer, no one could have been more
qualified to come to my assistance. We set to work at once to
try and discover what sort of man he represented himself to be.

Views about his notions differed widely. Was his art a
Christian art as was suggested by the titles of many of his paintings or did it express a body of transcendental views of his own
invention? The opinions of his few close friends and the wide
circle of his acquaintances differed. What about his desertion of
his first wife, Hilda Carline, and his second marriage to Patricia
Preece, alleged by some people (quite falsely, as we shall see) to
be a cruel scheming woman, who robbed and then turned him
away penniless, homeless, despairing? How did the other two
women come in? Did his art and his conceptions as an artist
turn on his relations with these women or was it independent
of them? Such problems, though subject to a desultory specula-

tion, were unresolved. The papers piled in front of us must contain the answers or what were they all about? In the interminable monologues which for years he had inflicted upon those he met, could it have been that he was explaining views, and recounting episodes, which the papers would elucidate? Even those who had listened with patience and thought they understood, had they in fact found a clear idea of the whole? His closest friends must have a notion of the truth. Or was there, perhaps, no mystery? After all a picture was not supposed now to tell a story; it was, in the jargon of the day, no more than an exercise in formal values. But not the most opinionated critic could have imagined Spencer theorizing in that way year after year. His paintings were not a mere dynamic display in aesthetics. He was using the force which a powerful composition affords, to give his notions vitality. But what precisely were the notions that haunted him, that he so wanted to spread abroad, but could not make clear by word of mouth? Would we find them entangled in the hundreds of thousands of words in the pads? What about the attempted elucidation by eminent critics, a Wilenski, a Newton, a Rothenstein in particular? Had they divined the truth without reading his papers? If so, why did Spencer impress on everyone the value of the pads, the necessity to preserve them, his desire for a biography founded on their contents and written by somebody other than the aforesaid commentators?

I plunged into the work along with my daughter. As we read, a story took shape; gradually, slowly what inspired his paintings grew clear. The fulcrum of his thought was revealed. As I read I kept in touch with Astor, Tooth and his two assistant trustees, informing them in particular of the curious sex preoccupation that pervaded the whole. What I said did not seem to them as fundamental as it was. If there was an erotic aspect, it was of small moment, they urged. But as my investigation into his account of himself progressed I perceived that sex was the main theme. In arriving at this conclusion I was greatly helped by the information given me by two persons, the most uninhibited of his close friends, Daphne Charlton and the pianist, Francis Davies. Both these persons were extremely fond of him.

They took me into their confidence. What they told me was supported by what he himself recorded in the pads. They did not know all that was in them nor were they able fully to grasp the totality of his thought, but what they said helped me greatly to find my way through the labyrinth of his papers.

The sex impulse which governed him was of a complicated nature. He was not indifferent to sex as usually understood, but it did not give him the maximum pleasure. As he grew into middle age he discovered deviations which pleased him more and which so dominated his imagination as to demand expression in his painting. Under their stimulus his paintings became more powerful and original. He grew into a potent and extraordinary artist. In his landscapes and his portraits there was no trace of these other preoccupations. That was the reason why he found them such dull work. He had to do them to make his living. Tooth was always urging him, demanding new landscapes because he could sell them. For Spencer they were drudgery. While his major paintings made it clear, once you had the clue, where their power lay, it did not seem to me that he formulated his condition clinically. What he did do was to invent a fantastic ideology, culminating finally in the worship of his dead wife, Hilda. It was the fact that she was dead which stimulated him. Charlotte Murray, the fourth of the women with whom he was on close terms, was by far the most intelligent. Indeed, she was the only person who really grasped his condition. By profession she was a qualified psychiatrist and after his death wrote to me that she might have been tempted to use her professional skill to turn him away from the sexual anomalies which pervaded his consciousness, had she not felt that to do so would have destroyed him as an artist. This view of hers was a most penetrating diagnosis. The principal sex anomalies to which he was subject were masochism in a variety of forms and necrophilia. The lesser irregularities were coprophilia and fetishism. His papers are very frank in these regards, and, of course, could not be quoted. His principal pictures are inspired by these perversions, but to particularize and point to these elements in them would require a lengthy inquisition, as would also how he sought to give them mystical significance.

179

Bearing these factors in mind, I wrote my first draft of his biography and sent it to Bill Astor. By that time I had signed a contract with Collins, the publisher, and accepted their advance in the usual way. Though I had endeavoured to keep Astor abreast of what was emerging from the pads, he was startled when he read the typescript. He could not dispute that what he now read came straight from Spencer's own pen. What he did not at once grasp was that Spencer's sex anomalies made him a more original artist than was generally supposed.

My next step was to submit the typescript to the three trustees, Dudley Tooth, Jack Martineau and Mr. Shiel. Not as well read as Astor and so less fitted than was he to understand what had come to light, their reaction was more negative. Billy Collins, the publisher, and myself were invited to a discussion in Tooth's office in Bruton Street.

When we were seated round the table I thought the trustees looked very glum. They could hardly raise even the smile that common politeness required. In a heavy, almost indignant, tone, they announced abruptly that they could not consent to the publication of the book. Billy Collins, however, was not a man easy to put down. He asked them to specify succinctly their objections. Their replies were weak and he dealt with them easily. He also pointed out (in a genial way) that all things considered an attempt by them to stand on their copyright and refuse permission to print might land them in a suit for heavy damages.

I supported him by pointing out that if my book was not published, someone else would publish a book which might be horribly sensational. There were publishers ready to offer a lot of money for such a book. A sensational writer could manage without infringing copyright. There were other papers in the possession of persons I could name which, handled in a popular manner, would appear far more shocking than the carefully balanced narrative I had achieved. If they attached importance to protecting the memory of Stanley Spencer from allegations in a book over which they could exercise no control, they would be well advised to keep to a book the contents of which were subject to their control. I had always from the start made it clear in letters and conversations that I would be guided by the executors' wishes and in submitting my book had understood that its text would be subject to amendment.

I also drew their attention to another matter which they seemed entirely to have overlooked to my surprise. An important theme in the book was where I showed that the damaging allegations made verbally by Spencer against his second wife, Patricia Preece, were untrue. They were prompted by his masochism. They have no place in his papers, not a word against her was recorded. Indeed, in the astonishing Temple of Love, which it was his ambition to see built and filled with his paintings, she was to have a chapel where she would be worshipped. I had promised to vindicate her. To go back on that promise at the instance of the trustees would be a disreputable act. So I told them and they winced.

On hearing these arguments and others, the three trustees abandoned their negative attitude with unexpected suddenness. They agreed to study my text carefully, note in the margin passages they desired cut or amended, and seek my collaboration throughout. For the additional work in which this would involve me, they offered an immediate payment of £400. Altogether, it was the handsomest capitulation I have ever experienced. Common sense prevailed. Dudley Tooth, moreover, wanted the book published. He had a large stock of Spencer's paintings and drawings whose value would be enhanced by the publication. I promised to sort out the drawings he had and explain their relevance and meaning. In return for this further task he gave me as a present a small pencil drawing on copybook paper which Spencer had made of himself and also two large important drawings, which he thought too indecent to put on sale, though they were psychological documents of importance.

As an example of the sort of high feeling that prevailed in certain quarters, I will cite from an entry in my diary made on 8th April 1961, a week after the discussion with the trustees. 'I was rung up by Patricia Spencer and her companion Dorothy Hepworth who described how a fervid friend of Stanley's had come round to their house, Moor Thatch, and tried to get in. Seeing who she was and afraid of a scene, they kept the chain across and only spoke to her through the crack. She was nearly in hysterics and incoherently denounced my book as a disgraceful exposure of Stanley Spencer. She had read it, she declared, though how she could have got a sight of the typescript I do not know, and screamed that the whole of Cookham was violently indignant. "I will write his life," she bellowed. The visit alarmed the two women in Moor Thatch, as well it might.'

Hysterical though the woman was, her attempt to burst into Moor Thatch and abuse Lady Spencer was a hint of the difficulties that might confront me, even though I had made an agreement with the trustees. People would press them to demand impossible emendations. They might threaten the publisher with an injunction. I reflected, however, that as none of them had read the Spencer papers, their total ignorance made them no more than a nuisance. For a person to denounce a narrative without having read the documents on which it rested would be a piece of stupid effrontery and could be treated as such.

My discussion with the trustees was on 28th March. On 13th June, having heard from Dudley Tooth that they had made up their minds about the emendations they desired, I called at his office. My contemporary note runs: 'Their copy of my typescript was handed to me. Tooth said he hoped I was not upset by the cuts. I came to the conclusion that most of them could be effected without unduly hurting the book, but that a few were unnecessary and some seemed to be literary criticisms with which the executors were not concerned. I told Dudley that I thought in certain cases his colleagues had gone too far. He replied that he would do his best to persuade them to meet my views. He then took me to lunch at the Cavalry Club.' My conclusion was that he had done his best to smooth down Martineau and Shiel, who remained to the end rather unhappy about the book, and I noted: 'I will now make the cuts and adjust my copy as far as possible to agree with theirs and send it in to the publishers to get on with the production.' In these terms I summed up the situation. In plain fact the emendations did somewhat obscure my central contentions, as was inevitable. What was never understood was that in trying to make Spencer look more conventional and minimizing the importance to his art of the strange sex anomalies which were his inner self, they were belittling the phenomenal nature of his artistic personality.

Collins got to work. They made sure of their ground by engaging the prominent libel lawyer, Anthony Rubinstein. He was obliged to advise further cuts. That and a certain timidity on the part of the staff at Collins led to more emendations. If I say that when it was published in April 1962 the book was not as penetrating a study of Stanley Spencer as it was in my first draft, I will, I trust, not be accused of conceit.

The book had a good reception. The *Sunday Times*, after hailing it as 'one of the most startling books of our time', serialized it at length for a fee treble the amount earned by any previous book of mine. It sold about 10,000 copies. Mr. T. G. Rosenthal, now a member of Thames & Hudson's directorate, understood the book better than any other critic and wrote in the *Listener* what a pity it was it had been messed about by the executors and their like. How tantalizing that I had been muzzled! The book was a good book, but how much better it would have been had people kept their hands off it.

Bill Astor acquired a building in Cookham and turned it into a permanent gallery for Spencer's pictures, lending or donating some he had bought, and acting as chairman of the committee of management. I had a letter from him to say how much he liked my book and its interpretation of Spencer's art, to which he now entirely subscribed, though at first, as mentioned, he had shown some hesitation. He tried but failed to bring round the members of the gallery committee to his view. The majority were residents of the village of Cookham who had known Stanley Spencer only during the later years of his life, and become proud and fond of him. They could not see him as the mysterious and powerful genius his papers revealed him to be. They rejected his own account of himself, written with such labour over the years, and insisted that the object of his art was to depict Cookham and its inhabitants in a manner half realist and half mystical. As none of them had read his manuscript writings or were inclined to give serious consideration to my attempt at elucidation, they had no reason to alter their genial conception of the little figure they had seen scurrying about the village for years with an easy greeting for acquaintances. To show their loyalty to his memory they decided not to display my book on the bookstall inside the gallery. All this was touching, but misplaced. Bill Astor attempted to point this out, but, as he told me, finding them so set in their opinions, did not think it worth a rumpus. I entirely agreed with him.

22

Astor's marriage to Bronwen Pugh

MEANWHILE BILL ASTOR himself was entering upon the last phase of his life, a period ushered in with bright hopes but which ended disastrously.

On 13th October 1960, at which date I had begun to write the Spencer book, I got a phone message from his secretary inviting me to come up the next day at noon 'to drink a glass of champagne with Lord Astor'. I asked her what was the occasion. She replied that she was not allowed to say. I said: 'Well, I have guessed it.' She said: 'Don't tell anybody.' My diary goes on: 'However I had not really guessed it because I did not know whether it was to announce his engagement to Bronwen Pugh, the daughter of Judge Sir Alun Pugh (an announcement which had been expected for some time), or whether it was to be the marriage itself.' The more I thought of it, the more likely seemed the latter; the Registrar would be asked to come to the house. I looked round, therefore, for a present to bring up with me and came on a mother-of-pearl plate made for me at Mergui from an oyster shell of exceptional size, with the added attraction that when the plate was held up to the light an island scene, not unlike one in the Mergui archipelago, became, by a freak of the shell, visible in colour. At noon next day I presented myself at Cliveden with my plate, which I left in the car till I knew for certain what was going to happen. The hall door was opened by an under footman, who conducted me through the salon to the terrace, where he suggested that I should go to the chapel in the grounds, the mausoleum built by the 1st Viscount. As I stood at the top of the terrace stairs I was astonished to see down below Bill Astor walking arm in arm with Bronwen, and attended a few steps behind by a cleric wearing a wide hat and cloak. No one else was in sight. It looked as if they were on their way to be married in the chapel. Though still rather in the dark as to what exactly was happening, I felt the footman must be mistaken about my being expected in the chapel, and returned accordingly to the hall, where I found that a number of guests were arriving. It was then that I learned that the marriage had already taken place before the Registrar in London, and that in the chapel there was merely to be a homily and a blessing.

As soon as the bride and bridegroom returned from the chapel, they received the guests in the salon. I went in, shook hands and said I had no idea the wedding was that day but nevertheless had brought a little present. (I already knew Bronwen slightly, as on recent occasions when I dined at Cliveden, she had been there and we had had talks. Bill had even asked me what I thought of her and I said I had been struck by the look of humanity in her face.)

Over a hundred guests in the great hall were being handed sandwiches and champagne. Mr. Lee, the butler, told me there was to be lunch for a few and that I was expected. When I went into the dining-room Bill made me sit at a little table with him, Bronwen and her parents. Nearby at another little table was his brother, David Astor, and his mother, Nancy, now eighty-one years of age. During lunch there were a few speeches, the old lady making one of them. She rolled off her stories. In this way Bill's third marriage began.

When the honeymoon was over, I continued to be asked up to the house. There seemed no change in the Cliveden routine. The guests at dinner were much the same type as before. I was there on Boxing Day 1960. It was not a big party. Old Lady Astor was staying, looking rather pale but as sharp as ever. Bronwen's parents came and Astor's old friends, Lord Palmer and his wife, the biscuit people. The young Lord Gowrie was there too, a dashing and handsome figure. And I noted: 'Dr Stephen Ward, who has a cottage on the estate, was of the party.' Before this my diary contains a few brief references to Stephen Ward. I knew that he and Bill had been friends since 1950, the friendship dating from when he treated Bill after a nasty fall out hunting. He was a well-known West End osteopath and was credited with a magic touch.

A youngish-looking man of easy manners, he was quite at home in good society. It occurred to nobody at this date that he was destined within a year to be the central figure in a scandal of extraordinary virulence, fatal to him and very damaging to Bill Astor and others.

This dinner party gave me the chance of observing how Bronwen was managing the job of being mistress of Cliveden. When it came to the moment the ladies should rise from table, I watched to see how she was going to get her mother-in-law on to her feet. My experience on such occasions was either that Nancy called out across the table to her son that she wanted to get up and wondered why he didn't give the signal or, when asked to rise, refused to do so, saying she hadn't finished her dinner. The way Bronwen managed it was half to rise from her seat and leaning across Lord Palmer fix the old lady with her eye, the expression on her face being respectful but firm. It was exactly the right way to go about it. The redoubtable Nancy got up without protest.

When the men were seated again I found myself next to Stephen Ward with Bill and Lord Gowrie. Ward amused us by an anecdote about Picasso. A dealer was very keen to get a drawing from him but Picasso was not willing to sell at the moment. A day or so later, said Ward, they were all sun-bathing. The dealer went to sleep. Picasso stole up and made a drawing on his chest and stomach. When the dealer awoke, he found himself the possessor of a Picasso drawing which had it been on anything but his own skin he could have sold for a good price.

Bronwen had already told me how the news of her engagement to Bill had been received by Dowager Nancy. 'Bill first of all went into the boudoir to tell her. When he came out he was as white as a sheet and I said: "What's happened?" He said: "Oh well, you know the sort of things she says." However, when I went in she was very nice to me. She is always all right if you are alone with her.'

When I was saying goodbye in the hall, Nancy came up and said something she had never said before: 'Thank you for writing that book on me,' adding quickly, however: 'But of course I haven't read it.'

23

Field Marshal Lord Alexander

DURING THE FIRST three months of 1961 Bill and his wife were mostly in America. By April they were home again and on the 22nd I had a message from them asking me to dine. One of the guests would be Field Marshal Lord Alexander, who had liked my description of him in my *Last and First in Burma* as General Alexander, in command of the British army in 1942 when it had to retreat from Burma pursued by the Japanese. It had seemed to me that what happened on 7th March 1942 near the village of Tauk-kyan, twenty miles north of Rangoon, was the most critical moment in his career. I described the situation in the chapter headed 'General Alexander's Narrow Escape'. In a word it was this: he was surprised to find the road blocked by the Japanese, the only exit out of Burma. He could not move the block. Circumstances were such that the Japanese had it in their power to capture him and three-quarters of his army. But the Japanese, though in overwhelming force, did not attack. As I wrote in my book: 'Why did the Japanese let him and his army go when they had him in their clutches? At one moment his career seemed about to end in a Burmese jungle; the next he was marching on to a Field Marshalship and a peerage.' The answer was that the Japanese command did not realize they had trapped the British army and its commander.

The chapter in which these events are described is the most dramatic in my book. When writing it I had not been able to have a talk with Alexander, as I had had with Mountbatten, Hutton and other personalities, because he was away in Canada as Governor General. So I had never met him until I saw him standing in the salon at Cliveden. He was seventy years of age, smaller than I had imagined, his manner quietly charming to those beside him. I will quote from my diary entered the next day: 'When introduced I immediately said how glad I was to meet him, as having been so familiar with the terrain he had traversed in Burma in 1942. Dinner was announced very soon and I walked into the dining-room with him as he seemed anxious to speak to me. At dinner, however, we had not the opportunity and after dinner Bill took him aside to discuss refugees. Presently Alexander entered the salon and came up to me to speak of the new Dufy which Bill had on an easel. I remembered, of course, that he himself painted and had even exhibited sometimes at the Academy. Everything he said about the Dufy was true and refreshing. We then looked at Stanley Spencer's portrait of Bill which was close by. It has always been thought that this portrait was unlike him and I myself had thought so, but curiously enough a week before when I was speaking to him about the Spencer biography, he turned his face and I saw the exact likeness which is in the portrait. I said so now to Lord Alexander, who, however, felt the likeness was not good, but Astor, who had joined us, was impressed by my remark. No one had ever seen any likeness before.

'Having in this way broken the ice by talking to this famous soldier about modern art, I said something about the Burma campaign. He said: "Why, that was a disgraceful defeat! All I did was to extricate the army." When we came to the matter of the famous Tauk-kyan block on the road to Tharrawaddy and the north, he said: "I have had some bad moments in my life, and that was the worst. But the Japanese would never have got me. If we had failed to clear the block, I would have gone into the jungle by myself or with a few of my officers and we would somehow or other have got to Tharrawaddy." It was wonderful how he remembered the Burmese names after twenty years. He then gave me his explanation of how the road block came to be there and why no attack was made on the British forces. Needless to say, the Japanese had no idea that they were letting loose the future victor in Africa and Italy, the man in fact who with Montgomery turned

the tide of war and made the defeat of the Germans possible in
1945.

'We were standing all this time behind Bronwen's chair in the
little space between that and the portrait.

'Then, speaking in a quiet tone he said: "We were fated to meet
that block. Yet I felt that all would be well, something would get
me through." I said: "It was your own genius telling you; there
was nothing else that could tell you." He said: "There was something else. I was told by my angel."

'When this great man spoke to me in so intimate a fashion, I was
much moved.' (Later, at a luncheon alone with him and his wife,
given by the Duchess of Roxburghe, he spoke again of his
guardian angel.)

His wife now said: 'Alex, it is time to go home, it is very late.' It
was in fact midnight. They had driven over from Windsor. He
said: 'I don't want to go.' She said: 'We must.' He and I ex-
changed compliments. Then he was taken off and that was the
end of the party.

24

The genesis of the Ward imbroglio

IT WAS THREE MONTHS after this Cliveden party that there occurred, on 8th July 1961, the episode of the swimming pool, a
light prologue to a drama that developed most dangerously. The
usual weekend was in progress at Cliveden, the principal guest this
time being the Secretary of State for War, Mr. Profumo. Stephen
Ward was also giving a party at his cottage half a mile away on the
estate. He had a general permission to use, if vacant, the Cliveden
swimming pool, which was in a walled enclosure close to the big
house, and he chose that evening to avail himself of the permission. Everyone knows what happened. When Bill Astor
learned of Ward and his guests being in the pool bathing, he
thought it would amuse his house party to stroll over after dinner
and have a look at the fun. Profumo took a fancy to one of Ward's
friends. This was the commonplace beginning of a drama which
was enormously to excite the public. I was not at dinner on that
particular occasion, but if I had been I would have noticed nothing
beyond an ordinary frolic in a pool. That it was unsafe to have to
do with Stephen Ward and his girl friends would not have struck
me any more than it did the members of the Cliveden weekend
party. Bill Astor liked Ward and had helped him to set up as an
osteopath in Harley Street. That it might be dangerous to have to
do with him never entered his head.

I dined at Cliveden on 22nd July, a fortnight after the swimming pool episode. The guests were official or professional
people, men from the Foreign Office with their wives, a Stanley
Spencer executor and his wife, a whole family of relatives from

Washington and so on. Ward looked in for a bit before dinner and told me about his latest portrait drawings. He had some gift for getting a likeness. This all seemed quite normal, but behind the scenes an ugly situation was brewing, which the following year was to cause my friends much harm. It was rumoured that Ward, not content with his excellent position as Harley Street osteopath and society portraitist, had conceived the daft ambition to influence Russo-British relations. That he was a communist was not the case. But he liked dabbling in those sort of waters.

There was no sign of what was boiling up till the end of 1962. I continued to be invited to Cliveden and met there the usual round of Astor's acquaintance, members of London society, the universities, racing circles, the embassies. Old Nancy Astor was often present. These parties were apt to be humdrum on occasion, as Bill held to the Victorian notion that charades, guessing games, songs at the piano, traditional in his father and grandfather's time, were the way to entertain guests after dinner in the drawing-room. There reigned an atmosphere of extreme respectability. I never heard even a *risqué* story. I shall not forget how shocked the guests were on one occasion when Bill, turning over the pages of a portfolio of Stanley Spencer's drawings, inadvertently displayed two scenes wherein the artist, prompted by one of the less acceptable forms of sex deviation, depicted himself seated in the nude on a double earth-closet with a woman he was instructing in the transcendental significance of coprophilia. Bill had hurriedly to turn over the page. On such evenings the ladies would sit in groups gossiping about their children, their dogs and their horses. No drinks were served after dinner. Not till it was time to go did Bill fetch a glass or so of port or a watery tumbler of whisky. The butler or footmen never appeared with trays of glasses. Bronwen used to sit stitching a piece of embroidery. Yet rumours were to circulate that orgies took place.

The parties at Cliveden varied, of course; they were not always so domestic. But the variation consisted in that sometimes the guests were more than usually distinguished. On 21st April 1962 when I was there I found Field Marshal Lord Alexander and his wife in the great hall. 'She is', I recorded, 'a dark handsome

Lord Astor in his bath chair in the rose garden
at Cliveden, July 1965

Lord Astor with the children of his three marriages and his third
wife, Bronwen, on the terrace at Cliveden, July 1965

woman. At dinner I sat between the Marchioness of Zetland and Bertha Bentinck, the wife of the Dutch Ambassador, daughter of the Swiss millionaire whose collection of old masters has recently been on view in the National Gallery. She wanted to know which I considered to be the best restaurant in London—Quaglino's or where? That being a subject of which I have no knowledge at all, I told her that I would agree with her opinion whatever it was.' Lady Zetland I had met a few years back when her husband was still Lord Ronaldshay. They lived close by at Marlow. Since then he had succeeded to the marquisate and the enormous family house in Yorkshire, Aske near Richmond, but had not yet moved from Marlow. Her father was one of the Irish Pikes.

At the end of dinner, as the men left the dining-room, Lord Alexander's charm of manner was very noticeable. 'By age and distinction,' I wrote, 'there was every reason for him to go out first, but he didn't immediately do so, since as an earl his rank was below that of the Marquess of Zetland's. While he hesitated to go, there was a respectful silence, everyone looking towards him with quiet admiration and, by a slight inclination of the head, inviting him to lead the way. A hardly visible expression of pleased assent passed over his face. He went out as it were imperceptibly, as if it just happened that he went out first.'

Whenever I came across him I was always impressed by his personality. On 9th June 1962 when I met him at lunch at the Duchess of Roxburghe's house, I noted: 'On saying goodbye to Lord Alexander I was much struck by the expression in his eyes. He seemed to look into mine in a curious way, a look which I have never seen before in anyone's face. He is a very extraordinary man, so quiet. His face was suddenly illuminated. One was taken for a second into the privacy of his thought.'

Such was the atmosphere of Bill Astor's house just before every sort of indignity was heaped upon him as the associate of Ward and his disreputable circle.

On the Astors' return from America in June 1962 I was asked at once. They were drinking champagne in the salon when I arrived. 'Bronwen gets hold of the neck of a champagne bottle in an attractive way. She pours with decision. "Oh, but you don't drink this," she said and ordered me to help myself to whisky in the hall. At dinner I sat next to Lady Ford, the wife of the Queen's private secretary. The Duchess of Rutland had with her the little poodle, which sits under her chair and has a plate put down for it there. A very nice cheese soufflé came round before the end. Bronwen, who keeps an eye on things, saw I liked it and told me to go to the sidetable for a second helping. I told her the compliments Lord Alexander had paid her at the lunch with the Duchess of Roxburghe. "Well, that's worth something," she said. It was one of the pleasantest dinners I have ever had at Cliveden. Bill was in such good spirits, the atmosphere was so easy.'

He was always on the lookout to do me a good turn. A little before this time he happened to lunch at the Hongkong & Shanghai Banking Corporation in the City, when the centenary of that immensely rich corporation was approaching. The managing directors wanted to get someone to write a history of the bank from its foundation in the eighteen sixties. My name had been put forward. The bank's head office was in Hong Kong and the Chief Manager, Sir Michael Turner, had suggested that I be approached. The subject came up at the lunch and Bill Astor was asked his opinion. He said I was the right person and from his close acquaintance with my books was able to advance sound reasons. The directors decided to take that course and I was duly approached. The result was the most lucrative commission which has ever come my way.

Hitherto I had never been commissioned to write a book. All my books, including the Nancy Astor and the Stanley Spencer, were undertakings of my own. No one paid me to write them. I offered them to publishers who contracted in the usual way to produce them and pay me a percentage of the published price on copies sold, part of this in advance at the time of signature of the contract. The case of a commissioned book was different. A writer was engaged to write the book and paid a lump sum for his work, irrespective of sales. As I had had no experience of commissioned work I did not know what I might expect to be paid by the Hong Kong Bank. The work would be onerous; a grasp of international finance as well as an acquaintance with a wide field of Asian history would be required. It would have to be a long book, detailed and sufficiently authoritative to satisfy the banking world and yet be a readable and, if possible, exciting account of how the Hongkong & Shanghai Bank was founded after the first Anglo-Chinese war, how it grew up under the shadow of the Ch'ing dynasty and prospered, and how it fared when in 1942 Hong Kong and South East Asia were overrun by the Japanese. It would take some time to write. I thought I might ask for a fee of £3,000. Some of my books had made more than this figure, considerably more in cases when film contracts, serializations and foreign translations were added to ordinary royalties from sales. On my consulting Bill Astor, however, he said £3,000 was too little. The Hongkong Bank was a vast corporation. The book would be distributed by them all over the world. It would enhance their already great reputation and indirectly benefit their business. I ought to ask for £5,000.

On a day fixed I presented myself at the London headquarters of the Bank in Gracechurch Street, E.C.3, to talk over the contract with the managers and the Chairman, Sir Arthur Morse, who as a former Chief Manager had rendered great services to the Bank after the defeat of Japan in 1945. He was a personality, tall, jovial and bluff, speaking with an Irish accent of the most attractive sort, in fact most unlike the popular conception of a big city man.

After a discussion over the size and contents of the book and the date it was to be ready, I said I would be glad to know what fee I could expect. Sir Arthur asked me what I had in mind. I felt diffident about asking for as much as Astor advised; a fee of £5,000 seemed rather stiff. Nevertheless, I did ask for it. Sir Arthur demurred: 'I am sorry, Collis,' he said in his Irish way, 'but we can't agree to that figure.' He paused, and then said as it were apologetically: 'The fact is we have budgeted for £10,000.'

Everything went happily after that. I became very fond of Sir Arthur Morse, whose death soon after the book's publication I felt very much. Its reception in the press was good. I was grateful in particular for some compliments in a *Spectator* review by Arthur Waley, who had always been so strict with me before. Somehow or other he was impressed by my apparent grasp of far-eastern monetary and financial matters, a subject which, great orientalist though he was, he had never studied. It was as if he sought to make up to me now for having in the past reviewed my books so severely. But, of course, I had no real grasp of the silver exchange. That the book's exposition of financial problems was correct, was due to the patient guidance of the Bank's experts.

25

The Cliveden scene

THE ASTORS WERE AWAY in America from 27th February to 12th April 1963. On 16th April I dined at Cliveden and met such people as Rebecca West, Derek Patmore and Bronwen's parents, and on 27th April Boyd Carpenter, the minister. Bill and Bronwen seemed happy and cheerful. There was no mention of Ward though on 1st April the police had begun an investigation into his activities. From that date the Ward scandal began to be given wide publicity in the press of the world. Astor's name was beginning to be mentioned. But he did not seem fully aware that he was being dragged into a colossal scandal. On 25th May I dined again. There was the usual Saturday party, which included Tony Keswick, a director of the Bank of England, who had been so helpful when I was writing *Foreign Mud*, and Sir Philip Zulueta, the Prime Minister's Private Secretary. Bill seemed in excellent spirits, Bronwen too was lively. Altogether there was no sign on this 25th of May that an atrocious storm was about to burst.

On 7th June 1963 Ward was arrested for making money out of women, and all England and America were set agog with excitement. On 14th June is this entry in my diary. 'Wrote a line to Bill Astor to assure him of my friendship and to say I hoped he was not being worried. I feel that he has innocently become entangled in a drama with which he has nothing to do.'

I was in London on 25th June and again on 2nd July. The Ward case was the main topic of conversation. I had drinks with the Berties, whose view was that a witch-hunt was starting.

Other friends of mine, well placed to take a level view, declared there was no real case against Ward. The law was not framed to punish people of his sort. He was the playboy type. There was nothing about him suggesting the underworld.

On 6th July I had a phone message from Bill Astor to come up to dinner, and at 8 p.m. rang the Cliveden bell. My note runs: 'Bill came to open the door. He said: "You ought not to ring, you ought just to come in." As I looked at his face, while we stood a moment in the outer hall, I was moved by the expression of suffering I saw there. There was a softness, even sweetness, in his eyes, a look of gentle appeal, which in all the years I had never seen there before. I pressed his arm, and said: "I know what a horrible time you and Bronwen have been going through." He half closed his eyes and sighed: "Yes, yes. The only thing to do is to keep up one's dignity, go on as before and not engage in a public slanging match with those women. After all, I don't live like that, Maurice. Hundreds of people know exactly how I live, what my interests are, how I occupy my time, what I do in the public service, what my private life consists of. We are being pestered by the press, spied on; the press helicopters are the worst, hovering over the house. My best course will be to wait until the Ward case is over in the High Court. Then when all the facts are out and adjudicated upon, it might be the moment for a letter to the press. What do you think? Could you do it then?" I assured him that I could, and would do so whenever he thought the moment right.'

My diary goes on: 'We passed into the main hall where he mixed me a cocktail. After that I crossed over to the small salon, sometimes called the library, where I found Bronwen's parents, Sir Alun and Lady Pugh. He had my *Hurling Time* in his hand. Almost at once Bronwen came in. "Ah, Maurice!" she said, a little wildly, and wrung my hand.

'We went in to dinner. Bronwen said: "All this has been a test of friends. Some when asked to dinner or lunch have made excuses." And she added laughing: "There were some old friends who complained saying—we have come to you all these years, but you have never once invited us to an orgy. After all, I've been married to Bill since October 1960, nearly three years. Surely I would have noticed something if he had been living the way the scandal would have it. It was a great surprise to Bill when some of the people he thought his oldest and best friends doubted or went against him in the crisis. But I think I'm a fairly good judge of character and it didn't surprise me as much as it did him." '

The trial of Ward in the High Court began on 22nd July 1963. A couple of days before that date Astor had said to me that he thought the prosecution evidence was weak; it was hard to believe that Ward had committed any criminal offence, though he had certainly been very silly and rash. Should there be a conviction, Astor said he would pay for an appeal, which, his legal advisers told him, would have a good chance of success.

This was the feeling at Cliveden when the trial opened. It lasted eight days. I noted on 30th July: 'The Judge started his summing up today. The verdict may be expected tomorrow. The prospects on the whole do not look too good.' The Judge told the jury there was a case and that they must decide whether the evidence sufficed to bring in a verdict of guilty of living on the earnings of prostitution. Next day the news was splashed across the morning newspapers that Ward had swallowed a large dose of sleeping pills and was in a coma. He left a letter stating that he feared from the tone of the Judge's summing up that the verdict would go against him and preferred to take his life. The jury brought in a verdict of guilty in his absence. He never recovered consciousness and died on 3rd August. My feeling, as I recorded that day, was that he had been hounded to his death in a clean-up. I wrote to Bill: 'The whole country has been invited to enjoy the spectacle of Ward's misfortunes. In a way he was butchered to make a Roman holiday. There must be a lot of people who were shocked at the set against him made by the police.' Astor replied: 'I think your assessment is right. The sad thing is that he would almost certainly have got off on an appeal, as I gather the law was very doubtful. It has been so difficult to know how much to say and how much to keep quiet, but I think for the moment silence must still be golden.'

Some time later Bronwen described to me how Bill took the news of Ward's suicide. He told her, she said, he could not face the dreadful scandal any longer and that he was leaving at once for America. She begged him not to flee the country. Despairing of convincing him that such a step would be disastrous for his reputation, she rang up her father in London. It was then eight o'clock at night. Her father and mother immediately set out for Cliveden and arrived at 11 p.m. Their appearance at the hall door with their suitcases at that hour was a dramatic moment in the Ward imbroglio, and one which remains unknown outside the family. Sir Alun wrestled with Bill and before the night was over persuaded him to stay in England and face it out. The aftermath of the suicide was exceedingly unpleasant for him. He was accused of having let Ward go to his death when a word from him would have saved him. These and other as meaningless accusations were hurled at him. However, he faced it out, putting his trust in Lord Denning, the Master of the Rolls, who had been asked by the Government to undertake an inquiry into the Ward affair with very wide terms of reference. One hundred and sixty witnesses were called. He examined Astor thoroughly, saw all his accounts and read his papers.

His Report was published about 27th September 1963. In it he cleared Astor, finding that in no respect could he be blamed or censured, being completely innocent of the rumoured iniquities which in press and conversation had been bandied about him. Next day a statement by Astor appeared in *The Times*: 'The Denning Report speaks for itself and I note and accept its conclusions and propose to take Lord Denning's advice and say nothing more whatsoever.' On this I wrote in my diary: 'Astor's suggestion to me that I might help him, if necessary, to refute the slanders made during this summer need not now be pursued. I am writing to say how glad I am that all has ended so well.'

26

The end of an epoch

IN MIDDLE SUMMER of 1963 the Astors went abroad for a while for a much needed change and later stayed on the island of Jura, where they had an estate. By the end of October both were back again at Cliveden. On 3rd November I went up to dinner. Bronwen looked well. Her first daughter had been born. This and the recent publication of the Denning Report had helped to restore nerves so sorely tried by the events of July. Bill came forward to welcome me with an air of affection, rare with him, for he was not naturally expansive in manner. In conversation with Bronwen after dinner she said the late scandal would have a lasting effect on his prospects in public life. Too many were still unconvinced of his integrity: the malicious people who had romanced about his connection with the Ward world would not easily admit the absurdity of their allegations.

I asked about old Lady Astor, now eighty-four. Was she as difficult as ever? 'She's all right for a short time,' was Bronwen's answer, 'but if she stays the weekend I admit it's tiring. I had her entirely by myself last week when Bill was away and thought of asking you to come up and support me.' Nancy, however, had stood by them during the crisis. Despite her prejudices she was a woman of the world. She knew her son Bill and she recognized rubbish. Anyone who dared insinuate anything against him got short shrift.

On 28th December I was at Cliveden for lunch. Bronwen said Nancy Astor was coming downstairs in a moment. Would I take her for a stroll on the terrace for ten minutes or so before lunch came up? I agreed, of course, so when the old lady appeared the suggestion was put to her. The sun was out. Would she like a breath of air before lunch? I had a glass of whisky in my hand, at which she looked narrowly and said: 'I'm not going out with a drunk man.' But that was no more than a customary sally; she was delighted to go, though she hardly remembered exactly who I was. We stepped down on to the terrace and she began talking away on her favourite topic—her having had to vacate Cliveden. 'I hate coming here. You can imagine, after being chatelaine for forty years, it's not very pleasant to see the place you loved in other hands. I should have insisted on my husband leaving it to me for life. Though I don't like coming, still I feel I ought to come. Bill would be so upset if I didn't. It's not that I have anything against Bronwen. She is very gentle with me.'

I said, pointing to the flagstone on which we were standing: 'There is a photo in my book of you and Bernard Shaw standing on this very spot.' This set her off talking of Charlotte Towns-hend, Shaw's wife, and saying how much she liked her. 'She was just right for Shaw. She kept back, but actually she managed everything.'

In this way the old lady continued to run on as ideas entered her head: 'That hedge, there's something wrong there.... Why does Bill cover up the sculptures at the end of the Borghese rail?... That tree shouldn't be there.... What's that white on the path? Sunlight?...' She was bent and inclined to stumble, and took my arm as we descended a sloping bank of grass. But she had a story ready, a droll reminiscence. 'His wife came up to me and said: "What a pity, what a shame! Poor George is drunk again."' She mimicked the woman's intonation. It was very funny. Laughing we reached the hall door and were about to enter the house when two teenage girls appeared from the direction of the stables. They were wearing trousers. Nancy did not know who they were or guess they were daughters of one of the guests. She called out in a hoarse tone: 'What are you two doing here?' The girls took fright and without answering slunk into the house ahead of us and disappeared. I said: 'They seem very shy.' She said trenchantly: 'Well, naturally, in trousers like that! Who wouldn't be?' Lunch was on the table and we went into the dining-room. This was my last talk with Nancy Astor. She died four months later (1st May 1964) aged eighty-five.

On seeing the announcement in *The Times* I wrote at once to Bill. 'The news of your mother's death was a shock, though I knew her strength had been failing. The year I spent writing her biography brought me close to her. It was a happy time. She was always exceedingly kind and considerate when she received me alone at her flat in Eaton Square. I took great delight in the wayward play of her humour.'

A memorial service was held for her on 13th May in Westminster Abbey. Bill reserved me a seat near Bronwen's parents. At the Abbey door I found Mr. Lee, who had been butler at Cliveden for many years, and had retired when Bill married for the third time. He looked less sleek. He is mentioned several times in my Nancy Astor biography, in fact so often that one of her relations complained that I had recounted his doings to the exclusion of more fitting topics. There was too much of 'What the butler saw' sort of thing. After shaking him by the hand and telling him how well he had contributed to the interest of the biography, I was taken to my seat by an usher in tails. The Abbey rapidly filled up till there must have been present nearly a thousand people, including members of the Cabinet and of both Houses of Parliament. One noticed also humble friends of Nancy Astor's, for she was much liked by women of the working class both for her kindness and the flow of her repartee. At the end of the service Bill Astor and Bronwen led the procession down the aisle. The manner in which she bade farewell to the Dean at the West Door was, I thought, quite perfect. As I watched, Home, the Prime Minister, passed close to me with his fixed smile and slightly upturned face.

Three days later I was invited to dine. The Cliveden round of weekend parties had started again and a number of distinguished people were present including two ambassadors and the granddaughter of the French poet, Paul Claudel. Bill himself looked run down and tired. I was not sure whether he felt the death of his mother as a genuine bereavement. Certainly the funeral, memorial service and letters of condolence had been a strain. I avoided the subject, as at a party of the sort it was impossible to talk privately. But three weeks later, when taking me in his car from a concert at Claydon House he began speaking about her. There was no doubt that he had mixed feelings. I recorded: 'He summed up by saying that when he was young and loved her, he suffered very much from the unkind things she said, but when he ceased to love her he got to like her better. He also said that one never knew from day to day, even hour to hour, how one stood with her.' I asked him whether he thought she really loved her children; had she any emotional tenderness for them? He replied that she had not. Such was his view a month after her death. Nevertheless her death was a shock. She was part of his life.

His general health was not good. He had always suffered from high blood pressure and now, aged fifty-seven, this disorder increased. On a visit to America in 1963 he was given some pills said to be the latest remedy. The pills, however, made him worse. On his return to England his London doctor gave him antidotes. These did some good, but left him very tired. Yet, he was not despondent about his health; whenever I saw him he was in lively spirits. He had an electrical parrot, a novelty from America, whose feats of mimicry it amused him to show off. Inside the parrot was a recording machine and also a transistor, so that what it recorded it could speak. One night before dinner, when introducing me all round, he pressed the recording button, and then the speaking button. The parrot's eyes lit up and in a ludicrous voice it began repeating the introductions. I heard my name yelled out by the brute again and again. Everyone was laughing. It was a good joke. I said: 'I believe, Bill, that posterity will remember you for this parrot more than for what happened in the Ward mix-up.' This went down well.

But, as I say, his health was precarious. In September of this year, 1964, he was in Italy staying at Asolo where Freya Stark lived and suddenly had a heart attack. Bronwen brought him home. When I read this in the newspapers I hastened up to Cliveden to inquire. 'His lordship has been in bed for some days,' said the footman who opened the door, 'and is still confined to his room.' I asked to speak to Bronwen. He phoned and she came downstairs. She attributed the heart attack to his high blood pressure, aggravated by the American pills and all the worries of the previous twelve months. Rest and quiet ought to put him right. He would like to see me, she said, so I went upstairs and found him on a sofa in Bronwen's room playing with one of the baby daughters. He seemed fairly well on the whole. That he was entering upon a dangerous decline I had no idea. In fact, he had only another eighteen months of life.

A fortnight later I had a message that a party of Sheikhs from the Persian Gulf were invited to lunch. Would I come up and help. The Sheikhs wanted to see the Cliveden stud. Bill would be just well enough to receive them for lunch, but not to accompany them to the stud which was on the estate a mile away.

On getting to the house I found him in the library. He said he had been in bed all the morning and had only just come downstairs. The doctors were not pleased with the progress he was making. Three Sheikhs were expected, the heir to a small state near the mouth of the Gulf, and his uncle and cousin. Oil had been struck there four years before and the ruler was getting £25m. a year already. They would have interpreters with them and a Turkish lady called the Princess Feuzi, who resided in London.

They arrived, dressed in the costume of their country, looking as if they had come straight out of the desert. Though exceedingly rich on account of the oil, their clothes were simple cotton robes, their head-dresses without ornaments. Their manner was dignified and rather severe. A lively little boy of seven, the son of the heir, was with them.

We sat down to lunch. My duty was to look after the cousin, while Bronwen took on the heir and the uncle. She had the interpreters handy and was able to keep some sort of a conversation going, but I had no one to help me with the cousin and could only pass him the salt and press him to have second helpings. Bill made no effort to do more than smile. He was much too tired to struggle to converse. The Sheikhs knew not one single word of English. They maintained an air of grave dignity. To what inquiries were made, they replied in Arabic. The tension was relieved by two homely irregularities on their part. The moment we sat down to lunch, the small boy saw some bananas on a dessert plate in the middle of the table and called across to his uncle that he wanted one. Though I think his uncle felt instinctively that this was a little out of order, he picked a banana off the bunch and handed it to his nephew across the flowers. The boy peeled it at once and gobbled it down and was ready when the first course arrived. The Princess Feuzi felt she ought to put in a word of palliation. 'I took him to the zoo yesterday,' she said. 'He was quite good and only asked for one toy during the whole day.' The other irregularity was that after each course the three Sheikhs got out their pipes, lit them, took one puff and then put them down.

At the end of lunch Bill asked me to show the cousin the grand salon. When I took him in, he looked round a moment and then raised his two hands in an eloquent gesture of admiration.

The moment had now arrived for the visit to the stud. As Bill was not well enough to go, he said goodbye, declaring himself much honoured by the visit. This was just right for translation into court Arabic. He then went back to bed.

At the stud the bloodstock was paraded, yearlings, foals and mares. Bronwen read out the pedigrees from the stud book, which the Sheikhs seemed to follow, when translated, for like most desert Arabs they knew a great deal about bloodstock. Very satisfied with the display they embarked on their cars and were driven off to London. I said to Bronwen I had done my best, though I felt it was a poor best. She assured me I had taken the load off Bill's shoulders. The cousin sheikh would have been too much for him.

A fortnight later I got a message to dine quietly. On being let in by the butler, Mr. Washington, I inquired how Bill was. 'I believe his Lordship is slightly better,' he said, 'but he isn't doing much. Dinner will be in her Ladyship's bedroom.' He took me up to Bronwen's room, an immense apartment facing down over the terrace and furnished with a big tapestry, some old masters and modern paintings, including an Ivon Hitchens and a large Nathaniel Hone. I found Bill sitting on the sofa in dressing-gown and pyjamas. There was a blazing fire and near it the dinner table, laid for four, the other guest being the Duchess of Roxburghe. Bill, though evidently tired, did not appear ill. He was eager to talk and spoke amusingly of several current topics, in particular of Rab Butler's political future. I noted: 'After dinner he made me sit with him on the sofa for a little bit, but it was evident he was getting exhausted. When I remarked it was time for me to go home, he wanted me to stay a little longer, but presently got up saying he should get to bed, though it was hardly ten o'clock. Bronwen saw the Duchess and myself to our cars. The Duchess got into her Jaguar and drove off to London. I dropped down the hill at a leisurely pace. The autumn mists were beginning to assemble.'

During December 1964 Bill seemed rather better though his heart attack had aged him. He was downstairs for a Christmas party on the 26th. In January 1965 he was well enough to go with Bronwen to Marrakesh for a complete change.

The Marrakesh trip did him so much good that he decided to spend March in the Bahamas in the hope that Nassau would complete the cure. What was essential for his recovery was rest and quiet. Cliveden made him nervy and irritable, Bronwen said. His mother's presence still seemed to haunt it. Away from the house he was a different man, she told me.

On 16th April, calculating that he must be back from Nassau, I called to inquire how he was. The footman said he was ill in bed. I wrote a note of condolence saying I would like to come in when he felt able for a chat. I gathered that he had had some sort of a relapse in New York where he had gone after his stay in Nassau. On the 22nd he phoned asking me to come up for a tray-lunch.

Ushered into his bedroom, with its dozen paintings of the Cliveden racehorses by Munnings, I found him propped on pillows in a four-poster, and sat down beside him. He said: 'Going from the warmth of the Bahamas I was caught in a cold snap in New York. After the Bahamas it was too much for me. The change hit me like a violent blow. I was in bed for a fortnight in New York and have to stay in bed another fortnight here.' He was able, however, to conduct his affairs from bed through his secretaries. He assured me that he was not worse. He seemed confident and cheerful and when I asked him what he thought of my Hong Kong bank book, said that the discussion of the silver problem, which had so much impressed Arthur Waley, had put him peacefully asleep. I assured him I was delighted to know that it had at least that merit. After a few lively passages of the kind, lunch was announced, not a tray-lunch in his bedroom, but in Bronwen's room beside it, where Mr. Washington had laid a small table.

A fortnight later, 6th May 1965, I called to inquire again. The footman sent in a message and I was asked to come up. Bill looked very thin and worn. He was on the sofa in Bronwen's bedroom. She seemed a bit distraught and not quite her usual smiling self. Could it be that Bill was worse? I only stayed fifteen minutes. Bronwen took me downstairs then, and left me to help myself to a drink from the table in the hall. The house was completely empty, the great hall without a soul and nobody coming or going. The silence and emptiness were somehow ominous. I went home depressed. Bill was not getting better.

This apprehension was confirmed when I called to see him a week later. Bronwen told me that he had had a searing pain across the chest the day before I last saw him, which she had been too upset to mention. She had the feeling that he believed himself to be dying. She had seen this expression in his eyes. A specialist, the best in London, was coming next day. Perhaps a fresh diagnosis might disclose a more effective treatment.

My next call was on 20th May. Bill seemed very pleased to see me, but Bronwen said he had lost his appetite, which so far had been good. When he did eat he was sick. He was taking the maximum number of pills for his blood pressure. It was impossible to foresee what might happen.

But by 6th June things had taken a turn for the better. I found him downstairs. He looked frail and I could not feel he was out of danger, but at least he was better for the time being. He tired, however, very quickly and went up to bed again. Bronwen told me she felt the strain less, but doubted whether he would ever be able to revert to his normal round. A few days later, however, he seemed to be on the mend and went to stay a weekend with a

Maurice Collis, aged seventy, in his study

Gerti Deutsch

friend. The win of one of his horses at Ascot cheered him. But he was not really better.

He now took to going about the grounds in an electric bath chair which his father had used in his last days. On 30th June I accompanied him to a rose garden he was improving and took several photos of him, one of which is here reproduced. He did not look dangerously ill, but he had become an invalid. Bronwen was keeping up heart but she said to me: 'He'll never hunt again. Might as well sell the hunters.'

By 24th July when I next dined at Cliveden, the old atmosphere seemed almost back. Zara, dowager Lady Gowrie, had just died aged eighty-six at her residence, Parrs Cottage, on the Cliveden estate, which Bill let her have rent free. He was always helping people by such kind acts.

The dinner of the 24th was to discuss Lady Gowrie's funeral at the Chapel Royal, Windsor. Besides her two grandsons, the Earl of Gowrie and his brother Malise Ruthven, there were no guests except the Windsor organist. When I entered the library I found Bill having a drink with the organist and discussing the music to be played at the funeral. His son William, the present Viscount Astor, who was then nearly thirteen, came in. I had met him now and then; his manners were exceptionally good. As Bill was so occupied with the organist and Bronwen was not yet down, a drink was not offered me and I asked William whether I might go and help myself to some whisky from the table in the hall. My note was: 'He seemed pleased to be treated in this way as the grown up son of the house and begged me to do so in the pleasantest way.' Shortly afterwards we went in to dinner.

'When we got to the dessert course,' I record, 'peaches were handed round by Mr Washington, beginning with Gowrie's wife on my left. By the time the one dish made the circuit to Malise Ruthven on my right, the last peach had gone. I did not particularly notice this and when Mr Washington offered me pears I said I would rather have a peach. Though seated on the other side of the table, William noticed what had happened and immediately cut his peach in half and passed it over to me. I have never seen a more attentive and graceful act by a boy of his age.'

Considering how very poorly Bill had been, in bed mostly and unable to come downstairs, one was astonished to note his energy now. I congratulated him on having got to Westminster a few days before and recorded his vote in the Lords in support of the abolition of hanging. He told us now that he was shortly going over to inspect his stud in County Kildare. After Ireland he and the family would stay in his house on the Isle of Jura. I should not see them again for a couple of months.

The evening was wound up in an amusing way by the mechanical parrot. The Windsor Chapel organist played on the drawing-room piano a verse of 'Rule Britannia' to the music of Thomas Arne. The parrot was then set to replay it. This it did, its eyes blazing, giving the music a sort of parrot sound, which was delightfully ludicrous and impertinent. 'What a shocking bird it is!' said Lady Gowrie, making its wings flutter and its beak move, which it should have done by itself but its works were getting worn out.

Much cheered by Bill's enjoyment, for he adored the parrot, and his apparent improvement in health, I said goodbye, hoping that when I saw him after his change of air in Ireland and Jura he would no longer be an invalid.

In October when he was back I went up to see him. I found him in the library looking very thin, for his weight had fallen to eight and a half stone. However, his colour had improved and on the whole he seemed less tired despite his drawn face. He told me that Ireland and his horses had suited him, but that in Jura he had had a relapse and a specialist had had to be sent for from the mainland. I was about to leave when he said that the Taplow vicar was coming to discuss a service in the Cliveden mausoleum to be held next day, the anniversary of his marriage to Bronwen. The vicar arrived and they decided to go to the mausoleum, which is a short walk from the house. He asked me to accompany them, going himself in his electric bath chair. The mausoleum, built by the first Viscount, is on a bluff over the Thames, a small circular building, the interior, reminiscent of the tomb of Galla Placidia in Ravenna, covered with mosaics and Latin inscriptions. The first and second Viscounts are buried there, as are the ashes of Nancy Astor.

The arrangements for the service did not take long. I remember that the flowers had to be chrysanthemums to harmonize with the gilding of the altar.

The following day he felt well enough to fly to Amsterdam to attend a meeting of his refugee committee. The journey was too much for him. Bronwen asked me up for dinner on 12th November and told me he had had a relapse a few days before. His heart was fluttering. He was to go into the Middlesex Hospital. When he came into the room—it was Bronwen's bedroom—he was in pyjamas and dressing-gown and looked thinner, paler and more exhausted than when I saw him before he flew to Amsterdam. The dinner was served on a little round table at the foot of Bronwen's bed. He could eat practically nothing. In the course of it he found difficulty in breathing and inhaled oxygen from a tube. I tried to entertain him by speaking lightly of what I thought would interest him, but soon it was evident he was in no fit state to talk. He had to take whiffs of oxygen again and again. I said goodbye and Bronwen took me downstairs. In the hall she said that my visits cheered him up for a while. When his heart fluttered, however, it alarmed him very much. She was pinning her hopes on the Middlesex specialists.

I went home feeling that Bill was now very ill indeed and might be beyond rescue by the doctors.

He was five weeks in hospital. On his return on 19th December I had a message asking me to dinner. I found him and Bronwen downstairs in the little library. He was in his night things seated in an armchair. The doctors had been able to do something. He was rather better and more hopeful. I gave him a few trifles I had with me as Christmas presents, including copies of my books which he had not in his library. *The Mystery of Dead Lovers* I inscribed for Bronwen, writing that 'her kindness to me had been without bounds'. She gave me in return *The Future of Man* by Teilhard de Chardin, a writer in whose philosophy of religion she had found comfort. I was able to stay two hours. When Bill went to bed she said it was touch and go whether they could do anything in the hospital. Yet she seemed more confident. I said: 'When I saw him on 12th November I felt he was dying, but have not that same feeling now.' She said: 'He was dying. But I too feel the crisis is past. He must, of course, be very careful. We will stay here quietly for a bit. Then in March get away for a change to the Bahamas.'

I noted: 'That is how things stand. He must avoid somehow another relapse. It depends on the doctors' ability to keep his heart and blood pressure in balance with their drugs.' The truth was that he was mortally ill. His arteries were overtaxed. The course the malady took was deceptive; he still had periods when he seemed on the mend. That there was no mending his ruined body I could not bring myself to believe. My diary has: 'Bronwen had shouldered the whole weight of the household and faces the future with emotion but steadfastly.' She was further harassed by the serious ill health of her father and mother.

The new year, 1966, arrived and on 2nd January Bill felt well enough to put on a dinner jacket, come downstairs and entertain a few close friends. I was there again on 15th January. My diary has: 'Mr Washington rang up to say they expected me to dinner. A little later he rang up again to enquire whether I ate oysters. I said I did not. "I told her Ladyship that, but wanted to make sure," he explained. When I arrived at the house he begged me not to mention that he had rung up about oysters. He had not been authorised to do so, he said, "Her Ladyship might be annoyed if she heard." It was a family dinner, with only one other guest. Bill was apparently a good deal better and had ordered dinner in the Pompadour dining room. Young William and I were provided with soup. I kept my mouth shut about Mr Washington's phone call. All went very pleasantly.' Bill stayed up till 10 p.m. I began to think my fears were exaggerated.

I was encouraged in my optimism when I saw him towards the end of the month. I asked him whether he had regained any weight. Only a pound and a half, he said. However, he was very cheerful, in fact in high spirits, due perhaps to a couple of cocktails, which was more than his doctors advised. The dinner was exceptionally good; the pudding was a masterpiece and I said so, too loudly perhaps for politeness. But Bronwen said: 'So long as you shout out compliments no woman will mind.' I was so pleased about the pudding because at Cliveden, instead of pudding, Bill liked a savoury with three special beer sauces, which he called the Brigade of Guards, an excellent savoury but I preferred puddings. After dinner, when we adjourned to the drawing-room, I noticed the disgraceful parrot. Bronwen picked it up and said: 'Come out into the hall, Maurice, and to amuse Bill we'll think of something to say in front of it.' We went out and she said: 'As you liked the pudding so much, why not say something about that?' After pressing the recording button, she began: 'I hope you enjoyed your dinner, Maurice.' I said: 'I particularly liked the pudding.' 'Why was that?' 'Because it was a nice change from the Brigade of Guards savoury Bill likes so much.' That was the conversation we fed into the parrot's recording mechanism. She pressed the other button to make sure it was working properly and with blazing eyes the parrot repeated the words, though in rather a low tone. She shook it a little and we went back into the drawing-room. There were about half a dozen guests that evening. When the parrot was handed to Bill he pressed the speaking button. It refused to utter a word, though its eyes blazed. However, a remedy occurred to him. Imitating the parrot's ludicrous diction perfectly, he shouted: 'I'm an Irishman and I want more whisky,' a bit of ventriloquism that set everyone laughing, except one guest, a rather dull chap, who looked at me doubtfully. I don't know why.

This episode, proof of Bill's happy state of mind, encouraged me further to believe he was picking up.

When I saw him next it was to bid him goodbye, for he had decided a holiday in Nassau was now the right course and was leaving on 1st March. One saw how much he had suffered from his long illness. His hair had turned white, his face was thin and lined. But I did not guess that I should never see him again.

On 8th March I was in London. While calling on Maeve Peake she said casually that the evening papers reported the death of Lord Astor in Nassau. This was so sudden a shock that I burst into tears. She apologized for her abruptness saying she did not realize I was so fond of him. On getting home I put in my diary: 'He was one of my oldest friends. The Cliveden period is over. My life will be different.' I wrote at once to Bronwen and next morning early left the note at Cliveden, asking Mr. Washington to deliver it when she returned. The newspapers stated that the body would be flown back for burial in the Cliveden mausoleum. Mr. Washington was outwardly calm, yet deeply affected. 'What a thing for us all!' I said, pressed his hand and left hurriedly.

Bronwen was back on 12th March and sent me a message to come up. She had brought Bill's ashes, for he was cremated in Nassau. At the hall door I asked Mr. Washington who would be at dinner. He said: 'Her Ladyship's sister-in-law, the Countess of Ancaster, her sister Miss Pugh, and Mr. Phipps from America.'

I found Mr. Phipps in the hall, a charming man of the Virginian family to which Nancy Astor belonged. I asked how Bronwen was supporting Bill's death. He said that he had travelled back with her from Nassau and that her command of herself was marvellous. I heard voices on the stairs and looking up saw her coming down with her sister-in-law. She came to where I was with her arms open. My letter had shown how much I felt Bill's death. Laying her hand on my sleeve she took me aside and gave me this account of Bill's last hours. 'While we were dining with some friends in Nassau six days ago, he suddenly felt a violent pain across the chest. We all thought it was another heart attack. A doctor was sent for; and he too diagnosed it as a heart attack and at once gave an injection which relieved the pain. But soon afterwards Bill said he could not see me. It was as if he had gone blind. He kept asking—Am I all right? What is happening? At moments he seemed to regain his sight. I had no idea he was dying. Then he lost consciousness. By 2 a.m. his pulse had ceased. It was only then that the doctors realized that he had not died of heart failure, but that an aneurism which had formed on an artery leading to the heart had burst. His blood drained away. It might have happened any day in the last year. The arteries could no longer stand the blood pressure.

'It is curious', she went on, 'how his long illness mellowed him. He became easier, gentler. The last days of his life were the happiest I had had with him.'

An ordinary conversation was kept up at dinner. In the drawing-room afterwards Bronwen handed me the typescript of a character sketch of Bill, written by the novelist C. P. Snow (now Lord Snow), which David Astor proposed to publish in his paper, the *Observer*. It was felt that something more than the rather bald obituary in *The Times* of 9th March was required. The obituary had the merit of detailing Bill's many public activities, his charities, his rescue of Hungarian refugees, which earned him the Grand Cross of the military order of Malta, and his chairmanship of several hospital management committees. The Ward case was alluded to, but in too guarded a manner. His friends wanted a more personal tribute. David Astor apparently thought that Snow's character sketch was good enough. Bronwen asked me to read it. I did so and felt obliged to say I did not think it would do. The typescript was then handed to the Countess of Ancaster. She read it and in her downright way said: 'Throw it in the fire.' The other two, Bronwen's sister and Mr. Phipps, were then consulted. They both declared emphatically against it. Bronwen agreed with us. What was to be done? Could David Astor be asked to write something himself? 'It's not all that easy to tell David his business,' said Bronwen. He was one of the executors under Bill's will.

However, when he was approached he consented. What he wrote appeared on 17th March, five days later. He spoke of the humiliation an innocent man had suffered by a series of fantastic accidents. The mood of the public became that of a lynching mob. Yet with lonely courage he withstood vilification by former friends, though profoundly wounded and strained and in poor health. His death was hastened by the abominable slanders slung at him. The Ward scandal from first to last was an episode of which the nation should be ashamed.

That it was thought necessary two years after the event to write in this way proves how the set against Bill Astor still lingered.

The funeral on 14th March was held in the mausoleum and was private. Bronwen, however, was anxious for me to go with her to the mausoleum and at 6.30 p.m. on 17th March took me there. On the walk down to it I spoke of her brother-in-law's letter and said I thought it well done. No one would care to come forward publicly and dispute it. (No one did.)

On reaching the mausoleum I saw the many wreaths piled up

outside its east wall, a mass of flowers. She unlocked the door and we went in. In the letter I had written her immediately after hearing of Bill's death I mentioned how some years previously he had pointed out to me the spot on the floor of the mausoleum where he would one day be buried. The ashes were in an urn on the altar and though the funeral service had taken place were not yet interred. She now asked me to show her the spot, but I was not able to recall it exactly. It must have been next his father's grave. And there the urn was buried.

27

Somerville and Ross

THE THEME OF this book has been to give an idea of how, after twenty years in the Indian Civil Service, I managed to make my way as a writer in London. Astor helped me by putting subjects in my way, particularly in the case of my Stanley Spencer biography. Moreover, his frequent invitations to Cliveden introduced me to a variety of well-known people. His death in 1966 was the end of an epoch in my life. I had reached the age of seventy-seven. At that age one can hardly expect a fresh run of luck.

Yet that is what happened. During the crisis at Cliveden I had not been idle. My *Raffles* for instance was published in 1966. The public found it a neat little biography. Even the Japanese translated it. But the main piece of luck was a letter from Nevill Coghill, Merton professor of English Literature, which I received two months before Astor's death. In it he told me that he and his brother, the baronet, Sir Patrick Coghill, had all their aunt's papers. Their aunt was no less a person than Edith Somerville, who along with her friend Violet Martin, whose pen name was Martin Ross, wrote *Some Experiences of an Irish R.M.* and other books. Published seventy years ago they still have a large and devoted public. Nevill Coghill's proposal was that I should write the biography of these two Irishwomen, basing my text on their diaries and letters in his possession. I went to his house in Gloucestershire, had a look at the papers, saw they were of exceptional interest and agreed to write the book. They turned out even more interesting than expected. *Somerville and Ross* was published in May 1968.

I was very delighted when Fabers decided to give a party in Dublin on the day of publication. The *Irish Times* was serializing the book. Edith Somerville and Martin Ross had been over-shadowed by Yeats and his circle. They were not held to have contributed to the Irish literary movement. The Coghill papers showed that their position had to be reconsidered. They were a product of the national genius.

Writing the book took me back to my youth. Ireland had been my home till I was twenty-three. After the long break of the First World War, which detained me in the East for six years, I made frequent visits. The Irish public had shown some interest in my books, though these had nothing to do with Ireland. *Somerville amd Ross*, however, was a different matter. Faber & Faber's party, given at the Kildare Street club, was largely attended. My surviving relatives and friends all came. It amounted to a reunion in very pleasant circumstances. I was able to visit some of the places in the Wicklow mountains, like Glendalough, with its black lake and Round Tower, which I had always found more beautiful than any of the fabled panoramas of the East. It began to seem that *Somerville and Ross* symbolized a return to my origins and might fittingly be my last book. But now in my eighty-first year I publish the present one with which, it may be, I take my farewell.

INDEX

Index